A FIRESIDE BOOK

Published by Simon and Schuster

New York London Toronto Sydney Tokyo Singapore

LINDA GEORGIAN
&
TAFFY GOULD McCALLUM

CREATE
Your Own
FUTURE

A Practical Guide

to Developing Your Psychic

and Spiritual Powers

FIRESIDE
Rockefeller Center
1230 Avenue of the Americas
New York, NY 10020

The information presented here is based on private research and is published solely for informational and educational purposes and is not intended for diagnosis or prescribing. Before you use any information or suggestions presented here, please make sure that you consult with your own personal physician.

FIRESIDE and colophon are registered trademarks
of Simon & Schuster Inc.

Designed by Jennifer Ann Daddio

Manufactured in the United States of America

1 3 5 7 9 10 8 6 4 2

Library of Congress Cataloging-in-Publication Data

Georgian, Linda M.
Create your own future : a practical guide to developing your
psychic and spiritual powers / Linda Georgian & Taffy Gould.
p.   cm.
Includes bibliographical references and index.
1. Success—Psychic aspects.   2. Parapsychology.   3. Occultism.
4. Georgian, Linda M.   I. Gould, Taffy.   II. Title.
BF1045.S83G46   1996
131—dc20   96-15157
                                                                  CIP

ISBN 0-684-81089-1

Acknowledgments

My sincere thanks and appreciation go to the following people:

Darline Beck, for her devotion to my mission, her positive personality, her help in all areas of my life, and for being one of my life's brightest lights;

Evelyn Bue, for her belief in the project and for her excellent research and assistance in the formulation of our approach and execution of our ideas;

Donald J. Carrow, M.D., for his time, friendship, and medical expertise and for his understanding and explanations of preventive medicine and alternative therapies;

Marge and Irving Cowan, for their unwavering support and for their help in getting me my first television show—broadcast from their Diplomat Hotel in Hollywood, Florida, and for serving as ideal role models as creators of their own futures. They are truly two bright light forces in my life;

ACKNOWLEDGMENTS

Nina Diamond, for being a superb journalist as well as a close spiritual and psychic friend;

Ronald Drucker, D.C., for his assistance in the area of holistic health and for his many years of great friendship;

Tom Ehrhardt, for many years of friendship and support;

Greg Harrison, for his technological expertise in the area of Kirlian photography;

Randal Jurkas, for his belief in holistic principles and devotion to the preparation and indexing of this book, as well as for his excellent marketing abilities;

Henry Kinney, the late columnist of the *Fort Lauderdale News*, for getting me started writing this book and for all the beautiful articles he wrote about me;

Ted Levchencko, for his longtime friendship and for his knowledge of alternative therapies and preventive medicine;

John Nero, for the many years he was a human angel, guiding light, and unconditional, loving friend;

Sandra and Patti Post, my sister and niece, for their belief in the power of the mind, for creating their own destinies, and for their constant support;

Deborah Rowley, for being a spiritual teacher and good friend, and for her excellent assistance with this book;

ACKNOWLEDGMENTS

Marie Simmons, my mother, for her spiritual, healing, and psychic abilities, for always having helped me to create my own future, for her work with God, Jesus, the angels, the saints, and those who have passed on, and for continuing to be my guiding hand, especially now that she is on the other side;

Howard Simmons, my stepfather, for being my greatest "cheerleader";

Julie Summerford, for her expertise as a media specialist and her assistance as a journalist;

Bob Yarbrough, for his typing of the original research and for helping me to know that, even though he has passed on, he is still with me and helping me, just as he was—unfailingly—when he was here;

All the television production staff, for their expertise, dedication, and care in helping me create my own future;

And, in addition, to:

Lynn Franklin, my literary agent, for also being a close spiritual friend, one who will be with me for many lifetimes ahead;

Sydny Miner, my editor, for being not only a believer but one who is *in tune* with me, whose holistic vibrations and consciousness work in tandem with my own;

Taffy Gould, my collaborator, for her understanding of and commitment to the same principles as mine, for being "the writing hand behind my mind" and the Writing Angel I asked God for, and for her teamwork, research, and interviewing skills;

Finally, I would like to acknowledge and thank all those people who have been in and out of my life, in readings and in classes, whose lives I may have touched and who have, unquestionably, touched mine. It is because of them that this book evolved. There is not space, here, to name them all, but I hope they are continuing to create their own futures.

This book is dedicated to my mother, Marie Georgian Simmons, who passed on August 5, 1991. Without her understanding, love, and belief in me and my work I would not have achieved all that I have in every area of my life. Her strength, compassion, sense of humor, and spirituality made her the greatest influence in my life and in the lives of those around her. Her presence is always with me.

This book is also dedicated to those truth-seekers whose courage and determination have opened new doors, and to those who follow holistic principles throughout their lives.

CONTENTS

CONTENTS

PART FOUR: RELATIONSHIPS AND SEX

INTRODUCTION

Over the years I have given thousands of psychic readings to people whose problems run the gamut of all the emotional and physical concerns that plague mankind. People ask me, "Why am I sick?" "Do you see me making any money?" "Why am I having problems in my relationships?" "Why doesn't God listen to my prayers?" and so on. In response, I tune into those who pose the questions and give them an intuitive reading about what I pick up at the time. If a person is not happy with what I see or with what is happening in his or her life, then I state the most important lesson I can provide: "It is within your power to *create your own future.*"

The name and cover of this book came to me while riding in a car, enjoying the lush tropical scenery. In my mind I saw a rainbow leading to a pot of gold, an image we all can understand. The words *create your own future* came to me with the realization that it is this lesson I am here to teach: We *can* catch the pot of gold at the end of the rainbow! And this book will show you how.

Most people are surprised to learn they are actually in charge of their own destiny, and that by using the various techniques I shall explain in this book and adhering to God's physical, mental, and spiritual laws, they can bring their lives into balance and achieve their fondest desires.

God does not predestine a person's life. *You* determine your own life and make your own path with your daily thinking and actions. In this book, you will learn to do just that—determine your own destiny and your own future. You will learn not to think of yourself as the puppet of some predetermined fate, a helpless victim of circumstances you cannot control. Through simple-to-read, step-by-step techniques, I shall provide information that will, literally, *set you free* of all that troubles you, *set you free* to be all you wish and hope to be.

You will be amazed at how much you can accomplish with the powers of the mind, properly directed. All it takes is awareness, desire, faith, and the implementation of these simple techniques. You will find yourself able to actually *will* certain events to occur in your life, by sending out specific thoughts. Through repetition, thoughts become reality and, by your own free will, you can override and change any situation, just by thinking and acting differently. Odd as it may seem, this is one reason psychic readings done for positive-thinking people can sometimes be inaccurate: Positive people are always *improving* the circumstances around them and changing their future—thus changing their reading. For the better, of course!

Forget the idea that "what will be, will be." The fact is, it will be what *you* make it. No one else (not even God) can be said to have "dealt you a bad deck": You are about to learn that, in truth, you have dealt your own and, what's more, if you don't like it, *you can change it!* By following the suggestions and assimilating the information presented in the chapters which follow, you will learn to open the door to all life's riches, through understanding holistic principles and attaining mental, physical, and spiritual health. In doing so, you will attract what you most desire: love, success, health, happiness, power, wealth, and spiritual bliss.

The term *holistic* refers to the mind, body, and spirit as being one and whole. We are *integrated* entities, and only when all facets are in harmony do we enjoy true holistic health.

This book covers all the dimensions which, together, make a person holistically happy. They include the universal laws which govern the universe; the steps towards psychic and spiritual development; the way to achieve optimum physical, mental, and spiritual health; the necessity of healthy relationships to your well being; the importance of being more open and aware of who and what God is; and the realization of what your own life's mission or purpose is. Each of these areas is important; each is as a crucial member of a team. Everything you think, say, and do is connected, in some way, with every other part of your existence and being. It is all interrelated, so you must pay attention to the *whole fabric* of your life. This is not a difficult task; in fact, you will discover as you progress that it is the *natural* way to be.

Relax, open your mind, and get ready for the most exciting lesson of your life. You are about to learn the Secret of Life: You are about to learn how to *create your own future*.

Part One

MY JOURNEY

The secret of success in life is for a man to be ready for his
opportunity when it arises.
—BENJAMIN DISRAELI

For they can conquer who believe they can.
—VIRGIL

I just want to do God's will. And He's allowed me to go to
the mountain. And I've looked over, and I've seen the
promised land.
—MARTIN LUTHER KING, JR.

In the mountains of truth you never climb in vain. Either
you reach a higher point today or you exercise your
strength in order to be able to climb tomorrow.
—FRIEDRICH WILHELM NIETZSCHE

Chapter One

THE EARLY YEARS

THE RECOGNITION OF MY PSYCHIC ABILITY

I am often asked if I was "born with a veil" and if my abilities are a result of that special circumstance. To be "born with a veil" means that, at the time of birth, a part of the amniotic sac (in which the fetus has lived in the mother's womb) covers the face of the newborn. A superstition persists that those born with a veil possess extraordinary psychic powers, that they are psychically superior to the average person, and that it represents an omen from God.

To me, this theory is unfounded; it remains nothing more than a superstition. Many who were born with a veil don't even know it, and those who *do* know it certainly don't all exhibit fantastic psychic powers. It is also true that some of the most psychic and intuitive among us were definitely born *without* a veil. The answer I always give is, "Yes, I was born with a veil, but I don't attribute my psychic ability to an amniotic sac!" I have worked too long and too hard, developing this ability to a finer degree, to believe it is just a circumstance of birth.

I was born in Cleveland, Ohio, of Italian ancestry. Both sets of grandparents came from Palermo, Sicily. Growing up, I experienced all the excitement, emotion, and intensity typical of an Italian family!

My school years were filled with sports, social activities, and just about every contest I could find to enter. Winning academic and sports awards brought me the attention I craved. With all my many activities, I was a highly self-disciplined student, so my parents never had to force me to study. I realize now that I was a perfectionist even way back then, and I took great pride in my ability to stay at the top of my class.

As early as age twelve I knew I had special psychic abilities. I recall, in particular, one day when I noticed what appeared to be *colors* around a junior high school teacher's head and shoulders, as he lectured. A flash of the color green, then an airplane, and then the city of Philadelphia appeared to me to the right of his head. I had had no psychic training—in fact, I didn't even know what a "psychic" was—but I felt this was an event coming up for him and that it would be good. (The green light gave me that indication.)

After class, I went up to the teacher and asked if he were planning a plane trip to Philadelphia. He said yes, he was, and then asked if he had mentioned it in class. I said, "No. I just had a feeling about it." Later, it was confirmed that he had a safe and enjoyable trip.

As time went on, it became apparent that whenever I saw or felt something *to the left* of a person, it represented the *past*. Something to the *right* represented the person's *future*. This remains true for me today: I "read" people like a book, left to right.

I began to understand that the colors I was seeing around people were part of the *aura*, or energy field, surrounding all living things. I began picking up thoughts from others *telepathically* and became adept at the most common form of extrasensory perception (ESP), the feeling of "just knowing" something was going to happen. This occurred more and more frequently, and I was right most of the time.

In high school, when I knew the answer to a question the teacher was asking, I would concentrate on my name being called without having to raise my hand. A good percentage of the time my little game worked! Without even realizing it, I was sharpening my mental abilities through practice. In college, my roommates constantly tested me, asking what grade they might get on an exam or whether they would hear from a certain boy at a certain time. The more I used this intuitive sense, the more accurate I became. (Practice *does* make perfect!) And because I felt close to God, having grown up in a devout Catholic environment, I believed my faith had a lot to do with my abilities.

MY PSYCHIC DEVELOPMENT

After graduating from Ohio University in 1968, I moved to Fort Lauderdale, Florida, with my family. I had been suffering for some time from severe migraine headaches and was experiencing some personal problems with relationships. These problems turned out to be a blessing in disguise, because in searching for answers, I took the advice of a friend, who told me to see a local psychic, the Reverend Jewel Williams.

I had been quite hesitant, at first, about seeing Jewel, because of my Catholic upbringing. Jewel was minister of her own church, the Universal Church of the Master Jesus. I knew my faith did not allow its members to attend or even enter other churches, but my intuition told me this was the right thing to do, and that intuitive feeling, once again, paid off. Meeting Jewel was to be a turning point in my life.

I began by attending—with a friend!—one of Jewel's regular Friday night "message services" at her home. About thirty people attended. Each of us wrote a question and put our initials on a slip of paper, which we folded and put into a basket. Jewel would take one of the papers, put it to her temple, and read exactly what it said—

without looking at it! This is known as "billet" reading. (Many famous psychics, such as mentalist the Amazing Kreskin, are adept at this practice.) On this night she selected my piece of paper, called out the initials "L.M.G." and said, "*You* do this work." Then she added, "You will do this in front of millions." She also knew—intuitively—about my migraine headaches and said I should have my neck examined by a chiropractor.

Everything Jewel told me turned out to be accurate and a blessing. Her puzzling prediction about my life's work has been and is now coming true. Even the advice on my headaches—rather controversial at the time—made a difference in my life: The chiropractor I chose was a practitioner of holistic health, a subject that has always interested and influenced me greatly.

After that first visit, I returned to Jewel's house on many occasions. At the same time, I visited other psychics and attended seminars and classes on "positive programming" given by Science of Mind, Unity Church, Maxwell Maltz, Napoleon Hill, Joseph Murphy, Norman Vincent Peale, Anthony Norvel, Dale Carnegie, and others. This proved to be an invaluable combination: While different psychics sometimes told me things about my future that upset me, I learned in my positive-thinking classes that I could *change* my future by "programming" for what I wanted.

Putting the psychic predictions and the positive programming together, I decided to concentrate on changing the things I did not want to happen. I decided to *create my own future.*

Before you jump ahead to the How-To section of this book, let me caution you that some crises or problems may *not* be "programmed away" if they are necessary for our personal growth. The trick lies in learning how to trust what you are doing and what is happening. As some would put it, "Let Go and Let God."

Once interested in all aspects of psychic phenomena, I read every available book on the subject. I also became involved in astrology, discovering that I was a Libra on the cusp of Scorpio, with my moon in Gemini and Capricorn as my rising sign. It was fascinating to learn that many aspects of my astrological chart—based on the date, time, and place of my birth—pointed toward an interest in health and spiritual topics and my concern for the well-being of others. My chart showed a good combination of influences on what has now become my life's work. (Though there remain many in our society who are skeptical of "these New Age practices," in fact astrology goes back to the ancient Hindus and is based entirely on the science of astronomy.)

I began working on my own psychic development with a combination of prayer, meditation, positive-thinking techniques, and creative visualization principles designed to bring only good into my life. I continued to search for a way to test my faith and theories and for relief from my lingering migraine headaches.

One thing I began to realize, by this time, was the fact that my whole concept of God had evolved considerably, from what had been my early experience. Growing up as a Catholic child, I thought God was a man in a chair, with Saint Peter sitting at his right-hand side and Gabriel blowing his horn. I believed that, if we were good, we would go to heaven when we died, get wings, and be assigned a cloud. If we were bad we would go to Hell, where there was a lot of fire and we would be forced to shovel coal while the devil poked at us with his pitchfork.

I now know "Him" as a vibrating sea of intellectual energy, a cosmic power, an infinite intelligence—omniscient, omnipresent, omnipotent. "He" is infinite light, unmanifested, the Higher Power. I learned that this Higher Intelligence, which I call God, is known by different names to different people, and that although I refer to this Intelligence as "He," in fact it is neither man nor woman, personal nor impersonal. God is, for me, an energy, nondenominational, not limited to any religions, dogmas, ideologies, creeds, or preconceived ideas of man. Through my studies I realized we were all created in His image and should, therefore, not limit ourselves, and I learned to strive for an ever-increasing awareness of His all-encompassing light and love.

MY TRIP TO JAPAN

In 1970 I decided to go to Japan. At that time, I believed in reincarnation, and thinking that I had lived at least one previous lifetime in that country, I felt driven to find my roots there. My desire and need to prove certain metaphysical theories compelled me to go to a completely foreign land, where I knew nothing of the language or the people, and where I would be forced to depend upon the guidance of God, Jesus, and the angels for every move I made. The lack of itinerary would surely prove my faith and my ability to communicate with God.

This was to be a metaphysical experiment to prove that I could create my own future through the powers of my mind. I decided to program my mind for the things I wanted to accomplish, actively visualizing and reading my long list of affirmations. I spent many hours each day reading them to myself and aloud. (I recalled that, in Catherine Ponder's book *The Dynamic Laws of Prosperity*, she said the power of the *spoken* word is sometimes greater than that of the *silent* word.)

Much to the surprise of my family and friends, I abruptly sold my car, quit my job, and bought a one-way ticket to Tokyo. And— feeling it would be good to have a contact in Japan when I arrived there—I programmed my mind to attract such a contact before I left home. A few days before my departure date, I "saw" that I would meet an important contact for my trip in the Benihana of Tokyo restaurant, nearby in Fort Lauderdale. So I did not question it when

I met two Japanese businessmen there, who offered to call a sponsor family in Osaka they were certain would be willing to let me stay at their home! My faith in the guidance of the Infinite Intelligence was validated.

The month I spent with that Japanese family further solidified my belief in the power of the subconscious mind. Even as I went about the usual tourist activities—the World's Fair, the opera, the markets, etc.—my strict daily meditations, visualizations, prayers, and mental attitude increased my psychic vibrations to a much higher level. I began to hear a distinct humming sound in my ears, the first stage in being able to hear clairaudiently. (Clairaudience is the ability to hear messages from "the other side" as well as from your own higher self.) Since I had already communicated with these celestial beings through visions and feelings, it was increasingly important to me to be able to hear their messages audibly. But just to be sure the humming in my ears had no medical basis, I did go to a physician, who assured me there was nothing organically wrong.

When I felt it was time to leave Osaka, I took the bullet train to Tokyo. Arriving without knowing a soul in that teeming city, I sat in the train station and meditated, visualizing that someone who spoke English would come to me and help guide me to where I was supposed to stay.

Suddenly, as I sat meditating, I received an impression that I was in the wrong place. I was reminded that, just prior to coming, I had asked for the location of the largest U.S. Air Force base in Japan, wanting to be near a big hospital. The largest base, I was told, was in Tachikawa—exactly where my intuition impressed me to go from the Tokyo train station. I boarded the appropriate train and arrived, exhausted and somewhat dispirited, around ten o'clock that night.

Of course I knew no one in Tachikawa either. But I continued thinking positively, certain my needs would be met. Knowing this to be part of the testing of my faith, I kept repeating to myself, "I know Infinite Intelligence is guiding me to the right place. I believe thoughts are things and that I can create my own destiny."

Walking through the narrow streets carrying my absurdly large and heavy suitcases, I came upon a building with an upstairs bar. I had to get off my feet, and the noise and music drew me inside. Within minutes, a Japanese girl named Hiroko, who looked approximately my age, sat down at my table and asked who I was and where I was staying. When I explained my situation, she invited me to stay at her house for the night—in Tokyo! I had been guided all the way to Tachikawa to meet this friend. My programming had worked again.

As Hiroko worked at Tachikawa Air Force Base, I accompanied her there on the personnel bus the following morning. Knowing I needed another helpful contact for a place to stay in Tachikawa, I visualized someone approaching me to help. True to form, I met an American girl at the bus stop. She invited me to her home, where I was greeted warmly by her family, who provided me not only with a place to stay but also with passes that allowed me access to all the clubs and shops on base. For the rest of my stay in Japan, I lived with this generous family and volunteered with the Red Cross in the base hospital, aiding wounded Vietnam War veterans.

My work at the hospital was highly rewarding, and my experiences in Japan were educational, but after a year I once again became restless. Many of my theories on metaphysics and positive-thinking techniques had been proven and my faith had deepened, but I felt frustrated at not yet being completely clairaudient. Emotionally still out of balance and feeling still spiritually incomplete, I realized I would not find all my answers in Japan, so I returned to Fort Lauderdale in the summer of 1971.

MY RETURN TO THE UNITED STATES
AND THE TURNING POINT IN MY LIFE

Once back home, I went about the business of learning more about my chosen career as a teacher and lecturer on holistic subjects. Not completely satisfied with my efforts, I knew I could be doing even more to help others if only I could more fully develop my psychic energies.

One hot, humid night in Miami, I sat alone on the shores of Biscayne Bay, knowing I was facing a crossroads in my life. I knew I had much greater psychic ability than most people: I was clairvoyant, could read auras, and could feel the cosmic forces of the universe. I had even gone to the mystical Far East in my search for the truths that eluded me. I had prayed in gilded temples and ancient shrines, in remote churches and in great cathedrals. I had tried to learn everything possible about the positive and negative energies of all the people I met and had tested my faith in every possible way. Still, I was spiritually deaf. The gift of clairaudience was being kept from me.

In my heart I felt I knew the reason. I was a normal human being, a young woman who—like most people—sometimes was influenced by the frivolous lifestyles of those around me. I felt I had been singled out for a special mission on God's behalf, but why couldn't I receive more direct guidance? Knowing I had not put my whole being into the service of God, I began to wonder if He felt I had failed Him. I was desperately unhappy.

All I could do at that moment was pray. I told God I was choosing at that moment to release my life to Him, that I no longer wanted anything that was not for my highest good. I said to Him, "I no longer want to do anything except your Will in my life." And, suddenly, I found myself staring at the water with a new inner peace. The emotional catharsis I had experienced had calmed my mind.

The following morning I was awakened by a voice saying, "Linda, I want to help you." Startled, I sat up in bed—thinking I had been dreaming. But the voice continued. "We will be working with you, guiding you, and we will present you with many opportunities to help you in the fulfillment of your chosen work." My reaction to this communication from the Higher Self was pure joy and spiritual ecstasy. I knew God had at last responded to my prayers.

Since that morning of July 30, 1971, my life has been guided by spiritual beings, angelic beings, and the God-force. I can hear their voices; I can feel their presence. For those of you who doubt these forces exist, I can only show you, in the course of reading this book and putting its theories into practice, how to experience this communication yourself.

I realize that many of the subjects in this book are controversial. The topics of religion, psychic phenomena, and nutrition always raise questions (and, not infrequently, eyebrows)! Not everything can be proven by scientific theory, but life is not lived based only on scientific theory. If it were, we would be nothing more than automatons. And, in any case, some theories are simply ahead of their time. To take but one example, look at the area of herbal medicine and how long it has taken the West to recognize its validity. Herbal therapies are as old as civilization, itself; yet only in the past decade have doctors in the United States "admitted" their efficacy.

No one has all the answers to life's questions, but we should always remain open to new sources of information. I shall never limit myself to "accepted" scientific or religious theories, and neither should you. A close friend of mine, the late Dr. Ray H. Cameron, has said many times, "The mind is like a parachute: It only functions when open!" Many people have attained higher consciousness and greater happiness using holistic principles. Others never try. Will you?

Everyone has a mission in life, whether great or small. Some of us never realize or acknowledge our life's mission; others realize theirs quite late in life. My mission is not to prove that I am a great psychic. Rather, I believe that God has presented me with the opportunity to bring together and then share all the information available today on holistic health. It is a tremendous job, one I may never fully complete, but I am doing my best to compile sources on the subject, including my own original research, and to introduce this information to as many people as possible. I also work hard at setting a good example.

Spiritual advisers tell me I am destined for my particular mission. To me, this is just another sign that I am on the right track. Even when things don't go as I had planned or wanted them to, I know that something better will come along and work out—and it always does! In addition, the closer I come to my goal the faster positive things have happened. This is part of the synergism of holistic life, and a sign that I should continue with my mission. Occasionally I feel overwhelmed by the enormity of the assignment, yet it seems it is at these times that people "miraculously" appear in my life to help lessen the load.

As with any large undertaking—especially one involving the introduction of new ideas—I have encountered many setbacks and obstacles along the way. I have endured the anxiety of financial problems, the pain of migraine headaches, the emotional stress of broken relationships, the exhaustion of overwork, and the struggles of hypoglycemia. But I have allowed nothing to interfere with this project, as I feel I am doing God's will by working to help others and myself. My life truly is dedicated to completing this important mission.

HAWAII

One more special place must be mentioned in the story of my early psychic development. Having been ordained as a minister in 1972 after six months of study with Reverend Gehrling and the Universal Harmony Foundation, I moved to Hawaii in 1978, to study Eastern philosophy.

Eastern teachings have had increasing influence on the Western world since the 1960s, as they advocate a calmer, more peaceful life, one less frantic and frenetic and more spiritual and meditative. In addition to the beauty of the islands, I wanted to live in Hawaii because of the unity I felt with the people from other cultural and racial backgrounds. Those I met showed a great deal of receptiveness to the holistic principles of body, mind, and spirit. As I traveled through the islands, I conducted radio programs, held seminars, and regularly lectured at the University of Hawaii, all the while taking classes, myself, to learn from the Oriental and Polynesian cultures. The Eastern influence from Japanese and Chinese philosophy led me to absorb their spirituality through seminars, yoga classes, and fascinating discussions with people of many cultures, studying in many different spiritual and metaphysical areas.

In Hawaii I met and learned from a *kahuna*, a high priest, with great psychic powers. He lived at the base of a mountain on land he had inherited from his ancestors, and he gave spiritual readings by communicating with the ancient spirits. His healing was done with all the tools of Nature. As holistic and alternative therapies are such a large part of their culture and so widely accepted, I was able to learn about them constantly and on a daily basis.

Each day in Hawaii I learned new things and became even more aware of the direction my life was to take. It was an invaluable experience, one that has remained important to me as I live and teach holistically.

Chapter Two

<u>THE LINDA GEORGIAN</u>
<u>SHOW</u>

UNDERSTANDING MY PSYCHIC ABILITY

After I appeared as a guest on a number of radio and television shows in Florida, I was asked to meet with a producer from one of the major cable television companies. The timing was just right. Thirty minutes later, *The Linda Georgian Show* was born.

One of the first misconceptions I had to explain away (and still do!) is the idea that psychics are always reading the minds of those they meet. Sometimes—just to promote pleasant conversation—I ask someone, "How are you?" and the person replies, "Don't you know?" The fact is that, most of the time, I wouldn't know, because my psychic abilities can be tuned in or out. Spiritually, I am always tuned in for myself, and often I am "just given" information that's important for me to know. But as far as other people and circumstances go, I deliberately tune out unless I need to know something. Imagine how mentally exhausting it would be if I were constantly tuned in to the personal thoughts of everyone around me! Imagine how distracting it would be if my psychic channel were wide open when I looked out into an audience. I would pick up on everyone's thoughts and auras simultaneously.

I remember receiving a letter from a man who had attended

one of my lectures. I was pleased by the many marvelous things he had to say about me, but then he added that when I finished the lecture he was positive I was "picking up" that something terrible would happen to him. He said that when he had approached me after the talk, he thought he had gotten some very bad vibrations from me and felt I was keeping something from him. I wrote back that, by the time I saw him, I had already shut off my attunement and the only possible negative vibrations he could have picked up were from the people behind him, who were afraid I wouldn't have time to speak with everyone. I do try to be courteous and dislike having to turn anyone away. I then reassured him that I didn't see any major difficulties ahead for him.

Often, when I give psychic readings, people expect phenomenal predictions and dramatic changes. I can tell them only what I *see* psychically, but no more. I also remind them *it is within their power to change what is happening in their life, that they can create their own future*. I also tell them to be aware of the effect other people have on them. We should select our friends, associates, and loved ones very carefully. Being around negative people affects us negatively, just as being around positive, uplifting people affects us positively. The effect may be negative reactions, not feeling well, being unhappy, feeling miserable at work, or unconsciously mimicking the bad habits of those around us, but—one way or another—the effect is strong.

When I started doing this holistic work I sometimes became annoyed or even angry when people didn't believe in or understand what I was trying to accomplish. Now, I no longer try to "convert" people, believing instead that they will accept a more wholistic way of life when they are ready.

Many people think the word *psychic* is synonymous with the word *occult* and, therefore, connected with Satan. This is not true. The extraordinary, or extrasensory, perception that characterizes being "psychic" is available to all human beings. In fact, it is known that this ESP is quite active in young children; it simply must be re-activated in adults. *Occult,* on the other hand, indicates something secret and available only to the so-called *initiate*—a totally different kind of understanding.

No psychic is 100 percent accurate. A psychic's accuracy depends on many factors: physical health, state of mind, ability to block outside disturbances, spiritual attunement, and personal concerns. These all work for or against being a clear channel for psychic energy.

I do everything I can to make myself a clear channel, but I can only tell people what comes to me. If I don't get useful information, I will not make up stories. Psychics don't consistently get specific or full names. For example, if you ask me what your dog's name is, I probably couldn't tell you. But I could tell you if the animal is unhappy or unhealthy.

PSYCHICS AND HEALERS WHO
HAVE INFLUENCED MY LIFE

Through my own research and through hosting radio and television shows, I've met many people in the psychic field. Almost everyone I met had some influence on my development, but no one did more for me than the psychic Reverend Jewel Williams of the Universal Church of the Master Jesus. After our first meeting in 1969, when she told me I would be doing psychic work in front of millions, Jewel and I became great friends. She helped me to become more attuned, and I assisted her with the psychic message services at her spiritualist church. She also encouraged me to further develop my abilities and continue my work with the media.

Jewel was also highly impressed with my mother, feeling that she had extremely strong psychic ability.

Since Jewel passed on in the mid-1970s, we have remained in contact. She periodically communicates to me in either my conscious or my dream state, encouraging and supporting my holistic work.

USING MY PSYCHIC ABILITY

ANGELIC HELPERS

Everyone has special mentors and angelic beings who surround and communicate with him or her in subtle ways. I encourage you to meditate before making any decisions, either personal or business related, because the guidance from God and His angels helps us to make the right decisions. Of course, no one is going to receive all the answers. But remember that sometimes, what at first appears to be a poor decision can turn out for the best.

My own angels not only help me make decisions; at times they also protect me from danger. For example, once, as I was starting up to enter an intersection, my accelerator suddenly stopped working. My car wouldn't budge. At that instant, a speeding car came barreling through the red light. Had I gone ahead I might have been killed, so you can understand why I value my relationship with the angels. They are here to protect and teach and help us. There is nothing strange about being aware of them and being thankful for their presence and assistance.

MY BELIEFS AND MISSION: YOUR MISSION

Since my mission is most important to me, it has, at times, taken quite a toll on my personal life. Being in the public eye means my frustrations as well as my accomplishments are magnified. Sometimes, when I'm down, I wonder whether my chosen work is really worth all the pain and suffering. But then, when I think of all the people I have helped and how important my goals are to me, I persevere.

I have surrounded myself with holistic, positive people. Those who work with me know there is much more involved than simply having an interest in the subject. Dedication is mandatory. One of my meditations is that anyone who would interfere with the progress of my personal holistic mission be eliminated from my life and surroundings. I always ask that the truth of all situations be revealed to me. Fortunately, my psychic abilities frequently warn me of future problems so I can try to avoid them, just as I would take an alternate route to avoid a tornado. In this way, unhelpful and counterproductive people are quickly weeded out.

I have learned a great deal—painfully—about personal relationships. If a person does not understand or appreciate my mission, if he cannot handle the intensity with which I approach and further my goals, if he is not interested or compatible in a holistic lifestyle, it cannot work. In dealing with unhappy relationships, I have learned that it is better to release that person from my life, with no malice afterward, than to try to "convert" an unwilling and unable partner. As you will see in my discussion of the Universal Laws (part II, chapter three), I have learned that God always provides someone better. (See the Vacuum Law of Prosperity, page 119.)

When I am frustrated by a personal or business problem, I turn this *divine discontent* into something positive, redirecting that frustration or anger into my work and goals. It's amazing how much can be accomplished by transmuting that energy and redirecting it into something good. (See the Law of Transmutation, page 118.)

I also believe in catalytic action. I find I often serve as a catalyst, bringing people and ideas together that otherwise might not have connected. Almost everyone has been in what seemed a bad situation but served as a catalyst to something better. If this catalytic action were not present in my own life (when I met Jewel Williams), it would have taken much longer for me to get where I am. As I feel strongly about this concept, I am also a strong believer that something good comes out of everything. If you look back at your experiences, I'm sure you will find the same to be true. It may be difficult to focus on the positive when things are going badly, but faith in this concept will help see you through all your life crises.

Another of my beliefs centers around what I call "the bulldozer effect," which involves combining energies with others who have like goals. This allows us to move forward in unity as a greater force than would be possible if we were moving on alone. There really is power in numbers.

I have discussed my feelings about the influence of those around us, having found that when I have negative people around me, negative experiences tend to occur more frequently. When I eliminate those negative people, the negative experiences subside or are totally eliminated. I believe that, once you've made the decision to be happy and be around positive people, you'll find it is much easier than being unhappy. I continually send out positive energy to all the people in my life, including friends and family. But remember that happiness comes from within. Don't depend on others for your happiness; just allow them to enhance your own.

One thing I advise, and that I practice myself, is to pray for everyone, everywhere in the world and to accept the prayers that other people are sending out. This may be done both in meditation and in regular prayer. Just the thought of all the positive energy being sent toward you can turn a depressed mood into a happy one. Accept it and use it. And share it.

In the strictest sense, a mission is a self-imposed duty. Therefore, one's mission in life could be to make a million dollars before age thirty, teach the handicapped, or raise three children. I believe that most worthwhile missions are based on service to others.

Although some (few) people feel certain about their life's mission from an early age, most often the discovery comes after hours of contemplation, reflection, research, and experimentation. I find meditation and prayer essential. Always ask God to show you His will. For those who are driven by their individual missions, it is that spark of divinity within them (the Higher Self) that places the positive seed thought. If they are inspired or motivated enough by this to take action, then by doing so they are expressing God's will through their mission.

Even an atheist can have a divine mission, without realizing it or calling it that. It is not necessary to attribute a mission to God for it to affect the world in a positive way. Madalyn Murray O'Hair, president of the Society of Separationists (also known as the American Atheists) has done a tremendous amount of good work, in spite of her anti-God, antireligion beliefs and even though she has many outspoken critics in the religious field. Without her efforts, and the efforts of those like her, there would be no balance against religious zealots who feel everyone should think as they do. For example, there are today certain fundamentalist leaders who are becoming so politically active that they run for public office. Without anyone speaking out against these right-wing extremists and enlightening the public, these extremists could effectively eliminate the competition by stacking the deck (placing their political/religious supporters in key positions), thus controlling the political process. By their own admission, this is exactly what they have done in a number of areas of the country, where they are well financed and where people are unaware of their underlying political agenda. These people would just as soon do away with the constitutional separation of church and state and require that everyone adopt their way of thinking. It would mean the elimination of free choice. Let me hasten to add that this goes far beyond allowing prayer in the schools, which many of us have little difficulty accepting. One of the most hotly debated issues, in this group, is the teaching of "creationism": a strict and literal interpretation of the stories in the Bible, rather than scientifically based courses in biology.

Now you see the importance of each individual mission and how it can affect the world at large. It isn't necessary to believe your mission will change the world, and even if yours doesn't *seem* to, it does in an indirect way. Just be true to yourself. Each of us was born with talents we are meant to express. Life is full of choices and decisions, and everyone can choose to do good in the world. You simply never know whose life you will touch with your thoughts and deeds. They are like the stone thrown into the center of a pond, causing ripples that reach all the way to the other side.

I am reminded of a teacher who learned at a *twentieth* reunion of one of her school classes that a "C" grade she had given a particular student on the semester's first test made that student determined she would "show" her teacher why she'd always been an "A" student. At the end of her four years at the school, the student had won the prize in that teacher's subject area and said it was the proudest day of her life. And the teacher never had an inkling!

If one is born into unfortunate circumstances, where the realization of one's potential is limited, the only way out is to overcome or change these circumstances. Many say, "What will be, will be," and make no effort to change their destiny. I believe in the theory that God helps those who help themselves. I also believe there is always a reward for self-sacrifice, if it is done for a good cause. The more you want from life, the more you must work to get it. Always be as clear as possible. Stay on the right road with the right people around you. Have a goal for the purpose in your life, and work toward accomplishing it.

Never be afraid of knowing the truth about any situation. Draw upon all your intellectual resources and solve your problems deductively. As you become more thorough in your self-analysis, you will begin to realize the divine order in your life. Put everything you can into bettering your situation and simultaneously ask God to help. If things don't always go your way, accept it—knowing you have the option to make things better.

God does not direct misfortune into our lives. There are risk factors here on earth over which we can never have control. Other people's actions and even natural disasters can manipulate events in your life in a negative way. Random events you cannot control may even cause your life on earth to end prematurely. It isn't that you have necessarily created "bad karma." We all must accept the fact that the world is full of risks. This means you must do whatever you can to protect yourself from harm whenever possible. Commonsense things such as not walking alone late at night, having a security system installed in your home, and having adequate insurance coverage are important in minimizing personal danger and lowering risks.

Prayer and meditation are also important in reducing your risks. Visualize yourself surrounded with the white light of God's protection and healing energy. Stay in constant communication with your guardian angels and you will get subtle messages that guide you away from negative situations.

Once, the mother of a girl who had been murdered came to me for a psychic reading. She was angry and upset because God had allowed her daughter to be taken from her. By all accounts, the daughter had been a kind and intelligent woman. The mother felt hypocritical about going to church, because in the back of her mind she felt that if there were truly a loving God, He wouldn't have allowed such violence to happen. It's difficult to explain to someone enduring such anguish that God is loving and does not randomly select anyone to suffer. But even during the most trying circumstances, we must know that those random events have some ultimate purpose. Notwithstanding all of this, I still believe strongly that with faith, prayer, and common sense, you can avoid many dangerous situations.

You may already know your mission in life, or it may take many years for you to realize fully what it is. There is also the possibility you will not recognize it in this lifetime. The great leaders of the world are here on special missions. I hope this book will help you to recognize your own special talents and to make the choices and decisions which will help you discover your own personal mission.

While I work with God and His angels by living as healthy and clean a life as possible, I don't profess to have all the answers. I am a researcher, and I am always learning new things about life and spiritualism. I know that God is constantly revealing information to me, that He is not dead, and that He did not stop communicating with us two thousand years go, when the Bible was completed.

I am fully aware that, if I have a conversation with someone at a church and profess to have continual *revelations* from God and His angels, many people would be quite interested in what I have to say, but that, if I said I was a psychic and received this information *psychically*, the reaction would be quite different. This is due, in large part, to semantic confusion: If the person in question has a bad impression of the word *psychic*, the reaction to my latter comment also will be negative.

Religion has been the basis of many bloody wars, deaths, and arguments. There are mentally unbalanced people running around claiming to be Jesus Christ or a reincarnation of Him, claiming to be the planet's new savior, or claiming God told them to commit heinous acts. It is difficult to make philosophical distinctions among religions, ideologies, and theories and among psychics, teachers, and spiritual leaders. People who have had a positive, uplifting, spiritual experience feel strongly that theirs is the only right message. It all feels so real that it is difficult to believe anyone else could possibly have had an equally enlightening experience and received different information. There is no way of knowing what the truth really is until we pass on.

This book obviously is much more than just *my* personal spiritual/psychic experience. It goes far beyond just a spiritual revelation to encompass every aspect of life holistically. It is meant to improve your life with information which may change your destiny and make you happier. It may even be lifesaving. At the very least, it will be health-giving, since I believe the holistic way is the quickest way to achieve all the blessings of the universe.

I am not writing this book to prove that God exists. That is something each of us must discover for ourselves. I do know that what I have learned and experienced thus far is real, positive, and helpful in every way. Although I follow my government's laws and truly thank God every day that I live in a country where religious freedom is a constitutional right, I won't let any power but God rule my life. As far as I am concerned, my personal mission here on earth will end only with my passing into the next life, but while I am still here it is always evolving. The holistic movement, however, will continue regardless of my involvement and long after I am gone. My plans may seem incredible to those who do not know me, but I fully believe I will be able to accomplish almost everything, if not everything, I set out to do before I pass on. Friends often tell me they don't believe any one person could do as much as I've already done. I have always pushed myself as far as I could go, seeming always to have time for something else. When an opportunity arises, I jump on it. When I get an idea, I research it and either pursue it or drop it. If necessary, I write down the idea and pursue it at a later date. When problems arise, I work them out systematically, trying not to dwell on them. In all things, throughout the day and every day, I strive for balance and positive energy, knowing that God and my guardian angels are there to assist me.

In 1991 I started a 900 psychic telephone line that quickly propelled me into the national spotlight. In 1992 I became involved with Inphomation, Inc., another 900 company, contacting my friend Dionne Warwick, who agreed to co-host an infomercial with me. Since then, the Psychic Friends Network has expanded greatly and, I'm pleased and proud to say, has become the number one Infomercial and the most televised program in the country. Various celebrities continually appear with me along with a screened, tested, and verified panel of psychics. My goal is eventually to syndicate my own psychic/holistic radio and television talk shows, in order to reach an even wider audience. I know that interest in this subject matter is great and ever-increasing in all parts of the country.

MY DAILY ROUTINE

People often wonder how I live my daily life, and whether I practice what I preach. As my approach to earthly life is a holistic one, my daily routine involves physical, mental, and spiritual aspects and disciplines.

Whether at home or on the road, I follow a set mini-routine. On first awaking, I spend about twenty minutes in bed, meditating and planning my day. Since I am a high-energy person with a lot always going on, I sometimes awake feeling anxious. The meditation helps to center me and focus my energy on the day's goals. I visualize these daily objectives in detail.

I make sure to try to get an adequate amount of exercise each day—walking, jogging, biking, and using a StairMaster. I also try to have frequent deep muscle massages, to help relieve mental and physical stress and tension. During the day, as I work, I constantly check and balance myself. If most of my work is mental, I make sure the evening's activity includes something physical. I try to eat only when hungry and sometimes conquer my sweet tooth by pouring salt on a dessert before I can eat it—especially on airplanes!

Sometimes, during the day or early evening, I meditate again, using positive-thinking techniques and prayer to attract good things into my life. I seldom drink alcohol and take no drugs unless they have been prescribed.

During the day, I frequently visualize God, Jesus, and the angels working with me in all circumstances. I feel comfortable with Jesus because of my Catholic upbringing, but you can visualize Moses, Buddha, or whoever else you feel is there for you. It does help to identify with a person in addition to an abstract force. The spiritual visualization process makes us stop to realize that God is always with us, always working on our problems and difficulties. Whether you visualize at work, while driving, dancing, watching television, or at other times, the important thing is to visualize as clearly as possible. I do this several times daily and at night, especially when I am under stress. God communicates with me mainly through the thought transference process, as He does with most spiritual people. The information I receive is always a revelation of some sort, concerning a problem or a question. Sometimes the revelation comes through a dream or through a sudden realization. There are many ways in which God can communicate with us—through meditation, direct voice, inspirational reading, or other psychic/spiritual means. Paramahanso Yogananda, of the Self-Realization Fellowship, expressed it beautifully: "In waking, eating, working, dreaming, sleeping, serving, meditating, chanting, divinely loving, my soul constantly comes, unheard by any: God! God! God!"

Part Two

METAPHYSICS, MIND POWER, AND UNIVERSAL LAWS

A vivid thought paints a picture, and, in proportion to the depth of its source, has the power to project it.

—RALPH WALDO EMERSON

Progress always involves risk. You can't steal second base and keep your foot on first.

—FREDERICK B. WILCOX

Imagination is more important than knowledge. For knowledge is limited, whereas imagination embraces the entire world, stimulating progress, giving birth to evolution. It is, strictly speaking, a real factor in scientific research.

—ALBERT EINSTEIN

Chapter One

METAPHYSICS

UNIVERSAL METAPHYSICAL PRINCIPLES

In order to understand holistic health, it is important, first, to lay the groundwork from which this concept is built. The basis lies in a clear understanding of universal metaphysical principles. By faithfully and persistently applying these laws, you can achieve all the divine blessings the universe has to offer, whether material (such as a house), a quality (patience and forgiveness), or a physical need (freedom from pain). These universal laws have been in existence since the beginning of time and, like natural and scientific laws, will always be around. The difference is that universal laws are invisible and, at this time, can be proven only by personal experience.

Metaphysics is a word derived from the Greek word *meta*, meaning "going beyond" and *physikos*, meaning "of the physical plane." Metaphysics, therefore, deals with the invisible forces of the universe and has only recently become more widely accepted, as science continues to probe the unlimited potential of the human mind.

Different principles govern each area of life: the mind, the body, and the soul. All the principles, or laws, in this chapter relate directly to one or more of these areas.

MIND, BODY, AND SOUL PRINCIPLES

To be happy and healthy individuals, close to God and with highly developed spiritual abilities, we must be in accord with the wholistic principles of mind, body, and soul.

The Principles of the Mind refer to conscious awareness. Simply put, this is known as *positive thinking*—seeing the good in all things and knowing that all things happen for the best.

To "prime" the mind to function in this way, it is helpful to study such subjects as metaphysics, self-hypnosis (also known as *autosuggestion*), the psychic sciences, and positive affirmation. *Become aware of your thoughts, since they are what mold your future.*

The Principles of the Body refer to the temple of the living God. Any abuse of it will be reflected in your body, your mind, your soul, and your affairs: The more negligence, the more difficulties. The needs of the body are:

A natural, balanced, nutritious diet
Rest and relaxation
Pure water
Pure air
Exercise
Moderate sunshine

The Principles of the Soul refer to prayer and meditation. The spiritual attunement with God (the Infinite Intelligence) through a direct, intuitive, transcendental teaching process, is the highest and most accurate form of education.

Spiritual studies, transcendental meditation, classes in psychic development, yoga, and other activities of this sort will help discipline the self for soul growth and open up the body's psychic centers, or *chakras*, which house the psychic and spiritual gifts.

Praise the Higher Intelligence for all things, so that a greater awareness will be revealed to you and a healing of any situation can be initiated. God (or whichever term you prefer) is within us and has provided us with everything we need. Without praise to this higher being, any seeming progress will be temporary and there will be delays in spiritual progress. Radiate divine love to the entire universe, especially to those people, situations, or things that seem to irritate you. As you will see, *everything you put out comes back to you.*

The closer you come to meeting these principles, the happier you will become—mentally, spiritually, and physically.

Remember that to achieve the benefits (the blessings), we must meet the requirements (the disciplines). Nothing comes to us free. We have been provided with all the capabilities, but we must work to make the highest and best use of them, to reap the rewards.

A client came to me with an assortment of problems. He was in ill health because he smoked, drank, and was overweight. On top of that, he was having marital difficulties and was contemplating divorce. He was a brilliant man, but the problems were affecting his work. He was no longer able to concentrate, and he was losing his clients. I told him what to do, and he said he believed in the principles but he couldn't bear to give up his lifestyle. I explained that he needn't make all the changes at once, but that he must begin, little by little, and be consistent and persistent. He would accomplish nothing if he returned to his old lifestyle; in fact, things would only get worse. I explained that, if he made the changes and stuck with them, eventually they would become a habit.

Success lies entirely within you, within your conscious mind.

THE THREE PARTS OF THE MIND

There are three distinct parts of the mind, and it is important to distinguish among them: the *conscious*, the *subconscious*, and the *super-conscious*.

The *conscious mind* is our everyday awareness. It is the mortal mind, where everything begins. This is where most of us spend the majority of our time, since this level concerns food, employment, home, money, clothes, friends, physical love, and other necessities of life. Although these concerns are unquestionably important on this level, we must learn to not restrict ourselves to viewing it as our only level of existence.

To gain the greatest control of our life, we must understand the potential of the conscious mind. We must be aware of our physical self, of our emotions, and of our reactions to the world around us. Most of us recognize the importance of the right foods, sunshine, fresh air, exercise, and rest, for our physical self, but we must remain vigilant, as well, of our negative emotions. Keeping ourselves in a positive frame of mind is of the utmost importance. If you feel yourself turning toward negative emotions of any kind, pray, meditate, or do whatever is necessary to overcome and transmute these feelings.

Be aware of your reactions to various situations, especially when things do not go your way. Do you become stressed? Feel sorry for yourself? Become violent? Quiet? Do you internalize your feelings? Or do you take things in stride, relax, breathe deeply, take a walk or meditate, and transmute your reaction into something positive? It doesn't take much to realize that the second alternative is the preferred path, the one which will lead us to greater health, happiness, and success in all we do.

Something good comes of every bad situation. Positive things are a result of prayer. Focus your conscious mind on your goals and objectives, and you will find that, by consciously affirming positive suggestions, you are cultivating a growing response from your subconscious mind. *Everything you experience in your conscious state is impressed on your subconscious mind.*

The *subconscious mind* is what we call "instinct." (This is not to be confused with the intuitive mind, which will be discussed in the next section.) The subconscious is a memory bank of all conscious thoughts and actions. It has no reasoning power and will accept as absolute fact all that we consciously impress upon it. Be especially careful of both the suggestions you make to yourself and those which others make to you: The subconscious mind will do everything in its power to bring these requests to fruition. In my own experience, I have noticed that, as I continue to program my mind constructively (which you will learn to do), my subconscious mind has become even more sensitive to suggestions, both from myself and from others. I even have to be careful of making joking comments, because—when I do—I find they come to pass! (Don't say something like, "I'd give my eye tooth" for something, unless you can afford to lose it or are married to a dentist!)

Have you ever been with someone who felt fine until another person said, "You look sick. Are you feeling okay?" Suddenly, the first person begins to feel an illness coming on. The reverse also can happen: I have friends who say, "I can't get sick. I have too much to do, and I can't afford to miss work." They rarely become ill. In both cases, it is the power of the suggestible subconscious mind.

Sylvia, an acquaintance of mine, was madly in love with a man named Roger. When Sylvia wasn't with Roger she would spend her time taking care of her classic 1957 Thunderbird. She would wash it, wax it, condition the interior, and polish it. Sometimes, she would just sit in it, listening to the radio and daydreaming (about Roger, I'm sure!). Although Roger liked Sylvia, she knew he continued to see other women. She wanted him so much that she often made the comment, "I'd give anything, even my car, to marry Roger." One day, returning from a day at the beach, Sylvia discovered her car had been stolen. She phoned the police, made a report, and waited for a response. There were no leads, and the car was never located. About six weeks later, Roger started becoming more serious about her and, a few months later, asked her to marry him. It may have been mere coincidence, but I believe not. I believe her statements, that she would give the car away to marry Roger, influenced the outcome. But be cautioned that frivolous statements like Sylvia's don't always have a happy ending.

We can make use of the powerful potential of the subconscious mind with positive affirmations in the conscious mind. Repeat statements such as, "I am prosperous" and "I am in optimum health" and they will be impressed on your subconscious mind. You can also read, memorize, and meditate on positive things, to keep yourself constantly charged with a positive frame of mind.

Avoidance of destructive, negative reading is a wise idea. Choose motion pictures and television programs that are inspirational, uplifting, and constructive. You can automatically charge the electrical and magnetic powers of your brain by focusing on uplifting and inspiring thoughts. Those who watch or listen to violent entertainment imprint self-hypnotic impressions on the subconscious mind. As we are increasingly aware—studying violence in our society—these imprints are ultimately expressed in overt behavior.

I have witnessed this imprinting firsthand in my experience as an elementary school physical education teacher. Some children came to class playfully imitating the violence they saw in cartoons, movies, and television programs. At times, they actually injured their classmates with these imitations. It quickly became obvious to them that what was portrayed on the screen was not really fun.

Remember that you influence your mind by what you watch and hear, the company you keep, and the situations you allow others to impose upon you.

The *superconscious* mind—also called the cosmic mind, the intuitive mind, the perfect mind, and the Divine Mind Within—is a vast storehouse of universal consciousness and knowledge, unlimited by time or space. Sometimes information from the superconscious mind is relayed to the conscious mind in a flash, through an impression on the conscious mind. We should always be aware of this "voice within," as we can tap into it and be guided by it. Those who live a one-dimensional life and place emphasis on the purely physical and material are actually blocking the higher vibrations of the universe, and they deprive themselves of the benefits they might derive from these spiritual vibrations. The result of this one-dimensional life is a feeling of frustration, anxiety, unhappiness, and general lack of fulfillment. Such people are satisfied with mediocre health, work, and relationships simply because they lack the awareness of our unlimited possibilities in this infinitely lavish universe.

We should free ourselves and open the prison doors created by our negative thinking and lack of wholistic awareness. *We can build mansions with the unlimited material supplied by our higher consciousness.*

Tapping into this higher consciousness, we can develop supernormal powers of the mind and body and even perform astonishing deeds. History books are filled with the names of great people who have made effective use of this vast storehouse of knowledge, and risen above the limitations of space, time, and matter: Thomas Edison, Alexander Graham Bell, Guglielmo Marconi, Leonardo da Vinci, Moses, Mohammed, Buddha, Jesus, Joan of Arc, and Mozart, to name just a few. The intent and noble purpose of their goals made them reach out to the cosmic mind and draw the inspiration that is available to all of us through imagination, intuition, dreams, and feelings.

Make it a point to dwell on the spiritual and cosmic qualities on a conscious level. You will then impress upon your subconscious the existence of truth, love, harmony, health, peace, and faith, which creates a strong attunement with God. I make it a point, throughout the day, to focus on these qualities, to make them a part of my reality. It takes just a moment, yet it always has an uplifting effect. The fact that there is increased interest in the study of spiritual and intuitive fields indicates that most of us are seeking this higher level of attunement. Even within the scientific community, this *reaching out and receiving* has become an important facet of existence.

Chapter Two

MIND POWER

THE POWER OF THOUGHT

Most of us tend to give little thought to the fact that our minds are constantly active. We take for granted the stream of conscious thoughts that is part of our every waking moment. Actually, these thoughts are responsible for creating our world and all the events that take place in our lives. Everything we experience existed first as a thought.

The connection between thoughts and events is not always immediately evident, but everything that happens has a cause. And however remote or obscure, that cause is mental in nature. What you think *does* matter: It affects your life and the lives of those around you.

Consider the person who wakes up in a good mood and arrives at work in a happy state but is greeted by a coworker with a bad attitude. That coworker sends out negative vibrations—knowingly or unwittingly. Our happy person tries to remain cheerful but, by the end of the day, returns home depressed and unhappy. That's why it is so important to learn how to control our thoughts and how to use them to our greatest advantage.

To learn "thought control" (a positive, not a sinister, notion), you must learn to use your mind as a child learns to control his muscles. Needs and desires inspire determination. The task requires a great deal of conscious motivation on your part, but the more you practice, the easier it becomes.

Every time you form a thought it is radiated from your physical body much like radio waves from a tower. The more energy you give to a thought, the longer it will remain in the atmosphere. If you have several thoughts, the lesser one will be overpowered by the stronger. This is sometimes called the Law of Dominant Effect. Exactly how a thought is manifested depends on the intensity and proportion of energy you give to it. Since your subconscious and superconscious minds also influence you, you will find that your thoughts may not, in fact, materialize as you had expected. Later in this chapter, you will learn to "program" effectively for the things you want.

If a thought is about another person, it moves to that person and immediately discharges its energy on that person, whether negative or positive. Thought radiations usually do not convey the specific details of a thought but, rather, the quality that thought gives off. For example, a jealous ex-boyfriend could have thoughts of killing his ex-girlfriend for having another lover. Now whenever she thinks of her ex-boyfriend she gets a very disturbed feeling. On the other hand, if a highly spiritual person walked into a room full of people, the thought waves of that spiritual person would affect everyone in the room, although not everyone would have the same reaction. Each person would react according to his or her own vibration level, belief system, and values. The vibration of each individual would be raised by this person's presence for varying amounts of time. This response is not always an outward one, but there is always an effect—however minute—whether on the mental, physical, or emotional level. We all can think of people whose company we enjoy because they always seem "up" and make us feel good to be with them. Conversely, we may dread the approach of a negative person, knowing what a downer it is when that person enters a group or discussion. Children, whose antennae are especially tuned in, are particularly sensitive to other people's vibes.

Each of your thoughts has a raising or lowering effect on your total vibration. Positive people tend to remain so, even in the face of adversity. Their attitude is positive, they expect positive outcomes, and so that is what they find—what they bring for themselves. People who look at things negatively will create negativity around them.

I met a woman, Carol, several years ago, who had a basically pessimistic nature. She was aware of her tendencies and even began taking PMA (Positive Mental Attitude) classes to improve herself. But she expected instant miracles and frequently reverted to her negative side. Once, she planned a Caribbean cruise and was looking forward to getting away. She had dreams about how wonderfully romantic the cruise would be, expecting something similar to *The Love Boat*. When Prince Charming did not appear, she became depressed and pessimistic, even though everything else on the cruise was perfect. Carol's friends expected her to return from the trip in a great mood, but she told them the cruise was a total flop and that her PMA classes hadn't worked at all. A good friend took her aside and explained that it was Carol's own fault, that she had not given the classes enough time and had, instead, allowed herself to go back to her old patterns. After so many years of negative programming, the friend told her, it was unlikely she or her life would change overnight. Carol continued with her classes and redoubled her efforts to change her thinking. Two years later, she came to me a changed woman: I couldn't believe the difference in her attitude and lifestyle! She was happy, healthy, engaged to be married, and—above all else—*positive*. She had finally realized how destructive her previous lifestyle and thinking had been, and now that she was in control and positive, she was on top of the world. What a difference an attitude makes! Her total vibration was higher and now better things were happening to her.

We all live in a cage of thought forms that we have created by our desires, mental imagery, and deeds. Although thoughts may seem intangible and harmless to us, this is merely an illusion. Our thoughts are extremely powerful; we should always be in control of them. If we let them ramble on aimlessly or dangerously, we risk everything.

Thought power can be used to create situations and reach goals. Weak or confused thoughts will have little effect on our world, but clear, straightforward, and sincere thoughts, properly directed, can literally work wonders.

According to the laws of metaphysics, all thoughts are tangible and carry either positive or negative experiences. This means that we are products of our own thinking. Now you can understand how thoughts you had in the past can affect your present circumstances, and how thoughts you have now can affect your future. Psychiatrists have long believed it is necessary to re-create the past in order to understand the present. Now we know that we can *create the future* by what we think today.

It is normal to desire different things at different times in our lives. Your desires for a particular thing or situation may wane, and you'll forget that desire ever existed. But some desires are so intense that they continue on, searching for a way to fulfill that dream.

An old student of mine, Stan, heard me on the radio and stopped by to see how I was doing. We renewed our acquaintance and he told me an interesting story about a girl he had known in school. It seems he had an intense crush on her and had liked her since she moved to his town when they both were ten years old. Even through high school he fantasized that they would one day marry and have children together. He visualized the whole situation quite clearly in his mind. After high school, they went their separate ways and he lost track of her. He went on to college, married someone else, went to medical school, and became an obstetrician. One night, when he was an intern on call at the hospital, a woman from out of town came in ready to deliver her baby. When Stan went in to see her, he was shocked to see she was the girl he had been in love with all those years. His dream of having a baby with her came true, in an altered form.

Stan created his future with his mind, just as you and I do, each and every moment of our lives. At the time of death, each of us will have created our own heaven or hell.

I don't believe that heaven, purgatory, and hell are physical places. Rather, I think they represent positive or negative states of existence—past, present, and future—created by our thoughts, actions, and choices. This is not limited to just our life on earth; it extends to our lives after death, in other dimensions, as various states of awareness.

YOUR PROTECTIVE WHITE LIGHT

If you feel someone is sending negative thoughts to you, you can shield yourself by visualizing a protective white light surrounding you. When you think about yourself, that thought hovers around you, waiting to make an impression on the subconscious mind whenever you are in a relaxed or passive state of mind. We are all part of God's existence, and we can tap into this divine energy source by visualizing it as a brilliant white light. In fact, this is how many people perceive God. It is the same radiant light often used to portray God in works of art.

Be aware that God is always with you. In your mind, picture yourself in an imaginary dark room. The darkness represents your lack of awareness of God's protective omnipresence. Make a conscious decision to turn on the spiritual light in that imaginary room. You are in control of the light switch. Now if a negative force of any sort tries to get into the room, it will be impossible. Negative forces cannot break through God's light.

You choose to turn the spiritual light on or off by being consciously aware of it. If the spiritual light is off in your room (your life), then by turning it on, you can make the darkness and negativity leave forever. Darkness and negative forces are repelled by the light of God. The only way there can be darkness in your room is if you allow it to be there, by turning off your spiritual light switch. With that switch in "off" position, you will feel separate from God, though in reality you are not. Separation is only an illusion. *God is always there for you.* I leave my spiritual light on all the time, and so should you.

Even though God's protective energy is always available to us, we must *use* it to make it so. The only time God protects us is when we ask, as in prayer. If we have faith and ask for it and expect it, we will be protected. The amount of protection is directly dependent on the amount of faith we possess. A half-hearted request for protection will not be as effective as more intense meditation and prayer which is full of faith. But faith does not mean we should forego our own common sense, in the way we live. Common sense, and a sense of responsibility, are paramount in everything we do.

DEALING WITH NEGATIVE PEOPLE

As I have mentioned before, negative people adversely affect our health, emotions, state of mind, and concentration. They short-circuit our progress and interfere with our well-being, by emitting an undermining vibration which upsets our whole aura.

To counteract this type of negativity, first visualize a beam of protective white light near that person's body. Surround yourself with the white light as well, and then picture yourself actually hugging this person in a spiritual way. Ask God and your angels to assist you and then:

1. Back off.
2. Hear the person out.
3. Move in at his or her level.
4. Progressively move the person to a higher, more positive state, through positive verbalization and body language.

Only once, express the feelings you're picking up. If the person is very negative and remains so, release him or her and remove yourself from the situation.

DECISION-MAKING TECHNIQUES

To assist you in your decision-making process, it is worthwhile to keep a ledger of your personal debits (negatives) and credits (positives). This requires spending just five minutes each day, making a list.

On one side of your pad, list all the negatives in your life—the things that disturb you. On the credit side, list the positive things—those that bring you contentment. These entries may be habits, qualities, attributes, and/or feelings.

Let's say, for example, that you wake up in the morning and find it's raining. The rain means you have to cancel plans for an eagerly awaited picnic. Then a loved one calls with unpleasant news. By this time you are becoming depressed, and with the depression comes a splitting headache. But in the afternoon you get an unexpected call from an old friend whose plans were also canceled by the rain. The two of you get together for a lovely evening of dinner and a film you'd been wanting to see. The depression lifts; the headache disappears. A day which began negatively ends on a positive note. Your lists for such a day might contain the following entries:

POSITIVE	NEGATIVE
Mike called unexpectedly; had a great dinner	Picnic rained out
Saw an old film I've wanted to see for years	Mother's blood pressure up again
	. . . Depressed
	Terrible headache all morning

After keeping track of all the negatives and positives in your life for a couple of weeks, you'll probably notice some things about your personality you hadn't noticed before. For instance, do you usually get depressed when it rains? What is really causing those headaches? Are you under too much tension at work or in a personal relationship?

The next step is to make a more specific list of negatives and positives that include your personality attributes, your interactions with other people, and the way you look at the world. Include both physical and mental items, and above all be honest with yourself. Your list might look something like this:

POSITIVES	NEGATIVES
Nice facial features	Tendency to gain weight
Creative	Too shy with opposite sex
Play tennis well	Terrible money manager
Hard worker	

If the debits outweigh the credits, you have your work cut out for you! But, as I'll illustrate later, your subconscious mind can help you get rid of all those negatives in your life.

The same system can be used in determining whether a relationship in which you are involved is worth continuing. Even if your credit list contained fifteen items and your debit list only two, you have to evaluate how well you can cope with the two debit items. For instance, if the debit list contains infidelity and emotional distance, can you really be happy with this person? A serious consideration of such a debit/credit list may help you decide.

In making important life decisions, a simple list is not enough. More often than not, several alternatives can be combined to solve a problem. Sometimes we reach crossroads where a decision must be made amid much confusion. For these situations, I have developed a more extensive decision-making technique.

First, gather as many facts as possible at this stage of the process. Next, ask yourself which choice is most closely aligned to and supportive of your main goal or purpose in life. Considering immediate, intermediate, and long-term goals will enable you to make the best possible decision. Then, the next question you must answer is: Which choice has the best potential for the greatest good in your life?

Fear of making a decision should have no place in your life. Once you've made your decision, stand by it. If you based it honestly on the best information available at the time, then even if you are criticized for it you can absolve yourself of personal guilt by knowing you did what you really thought was right. *Indecision is probably the greatest waste of time.* None of us has time to waste. But there is a difference between indecision and taking plenty of time to make an *informed* decision. That's where being honest with yourself comes in.

MAKING A LIFE PLAN

Getting to know yourself better by compiling the data just described will help you develop your own *holistic blueprint of destiny.* This Life Plan, or Future Plan, is similar to a traditional blueprint: It is like an architectural plan for your life. Making such a plan will be a major step in actively creating your future.

It is best not to put any time limits on the goals in your Future Plan. Just work toward your goals and know that God, the Infinite Intelligence, is working it out in the divine order. Anyone who has tried to diet, setting both a weight and a time goal, knows the pitfalls of such a plan: Not reaching your desired weight in the prescribed period of time triggers a whole chain of negative reactions. Better to set the weight goal and know that, with God's help and the proper determination and perseverance, that goal *will* be reached. In the long-term, it is *reaching* the goal which is important. An extra two weeks or two months won't matter to your health, as long as you stay focused. And keeping a positive attitude will help you achieve that goal in spite of occasional lapses. As you list your goals and desires in life, include what type of mate you would like, the qualities and habits you would like to develop, the amount of money you would like to have, etc. Write down every detail of what you wish to bring into your life. Your list might look something like this:

1. I would like to attract the ideal job. I would like to
   be a _____. (If you really don't know what to do,
   then meditate on God's giving you direction. It's
   very difficult for the forces of the universe to bring
   you what you want if *you* don't know what you
   want. The sooner you make your choices, the quicker
   they will come to you.)
2. I would like a salary increase of _____ per month.
   (Make the amount of increase realistic. You must
   also feel that you are worthy to receive it by working
   to the best of your ability.)
3. I would like to acquire the following vehicle:
   _____. (Describe it in detail—the make, model,

year, and color. Don't worry about how you will acquire it. Just plant the subconscious seed and it will
eventually grow.)

4. I would like to attract the perfect romantic relationship or marriage. My ideal partner would have the
   following qualities: _____. (List the details: height,
   weight, hair/eye color, build, humor, personality,
   character traits, etc.)

5. I desire to have perfect health. I would like to be
   free of disease and discomfort. (List whatever
   health problems you want to overcome.) I would
   like to be full of vitality.

6. I would like to travel to (list places) and travel by
   (list modes of transportation).

7. I would like to develop the following talents (list).

8. I would like to achieve the weight of _____
   pounds.

9. I would like to live in a _____. (Be specific: rent or
   own; house, apartment, or townhouse; by the
   ocean, a mountain, a lake, a forest, etc.)

10. I would like to attract the perfect friends with the
    following qualities (list).

11. I would like to achieve _____ in my spiritual devel-
    opment. (List: clearer communication with God,
    psychic ability, healing ability, etc.)

12. I would like to rid myself of the following negative
    habits (list).

13. I desire to have an improvement in my family rela-
    tions. (List: I would like my brother and sister to get
    along better. I would like to communicate more
    with my mother, etc.)

14. I would like to attract $_____ (whatever amount

you feel you have the ability to attract) from unknown sources. (It is important to list what you
would do with the money.)
15. I would like to improve my appearance in the following ways (list).

Read your holistic Future Plan over carefully in the morning and before retiring. If you visualize vividly the things you want, just before you fall asleep, you'll probably find your dreams reflecting some of these positive thoughts. That's a good sign you are making an impression on the subconscious mind.

When looking over your list, always initiate the Law of Faith: *Feel* the joy of fulfilling your written goals and desires. *Trust* that something better will always work out. The more you visualize, the greater the response will be. For example, if you want a new car, vividly picture yourself calling your friend to tell him how happy you are with your new car.

Make a scrapbook of pictures that represent the things, places, and people you desire. This is another major step in the creation of your future. In addition, to be even more effective, you may want to list your goals and desires under each picture. Get a magazine and cut out a picture of the house you would like to have; go to a travel agent and get brochures of Europe, Japan, or wherever you want to go; put a picture in the book of the ideal physical body you would like to attain. This scrapbook will serve as a visual aid to your personal holistic blueprint.

In addition to your scrapbook, place the same pictures on a piece of poster board. Look at it every day and visualize yourself actively taking part in the pictures. Become emotionally involved with these pictures and see yourself in them. Place your goal board where you will see it often, so it can impress your subconscious mind with the desired goals.

AFFIRMATIONS: WORDS THAT HEAL

Once having completed your Future Plan and scrapbook, the next step is to list your affirmations. An affirmation is a positive declaration of something good you desire. It is written down, verbally decreed, and mentally visualized. When used on a daily basis, affirmations can work miracles. Affirming that you have already attained your heart's desires is the secret to actually getting them. As you faithfully continue to affirm your goals and desires, you'll see how quickly divine results begin to be achieved.

Repeatedly talking about how much is lacking in your life, instead of affirming what you want, only blocks better circumstances from coming to you. In her book *The Dynamic Laws of Prosperity*, Catherine Ponder calls this "hard luck talk." People frequently engage in hard luck talk, usually with others who join in with their own complaints. All this does is reinforce the seemingly uncontrolled vicious cycle of unfortunate events.

Spend at least ten or fifteen minutes daily on your affirmations, in order to activate their miracle-working powers. If possible, try to affirm with one or more people of like mind. This combined energy will help you to speed up the process in achieving your goals and desires. There definitely is more power in greater numbers.

When listing your personal affirmations:

1. Write them in the present tense.
2. State them positively.
3. Experience the feelings that go along with them.
4. Repeat them every day.

Following these steps will make your affirmations a permanent impression on your subconscious. It is important that your desires be aligned with those of the universe; therefore, always conclude your affirmations with, "This, or something better, is now working for my highest good."

To assist your subconscious, create two columns on a sheet of paper. Title the left one "Affirmation" and the right one "What Comes Up." Once in a relaxed state, begin filling in your first affirmation. Wait and see what arises from your subconscious mind. Write it down in the right-hand column. Repeat this process for each affirmation. You will soon discover the negative beliefs that may have been holding you back.

Since *thought* is the root of all your mental and physical blocks, repetition of your positive affirmations will soon replace the negatives and attract good to you. How long this takes will depend on the strength of your old way of thinking, your degree of motivation, and how often you repeat your affirmations.

In my own life, I am witness to the amazing results affirmations have made. I actively affirm throughout the day and suggest you do, too. As an example, here are some of my own personal/holistic affirmations:

1. I am attracting perfect health. My body is in perfect health—*now*. I see white light in every cell. I have energy, vitality, and strength. Whatever means are necessary to obtain this perfection are made available to me *now*. Thank you, God!
2. I exercise every day and feel better and better.
3. I am protected from all accidents, illnesses, misfortunes, and harassments.
4. I consciously, and by request to the angelic beings, send love and light to everybody, everywhere, at all times. The divine energy flows constantly.
5. I praise God for all things that have occurred and that are happening now. Everything works out for the best.

6. My resources are unlimited and are constantly growing.

7. God and His legions of angels guide and protect me all the time and bring me the perfect opportunities.

8. All my needs are fulfilled.

9. The closer I get to my goals, the faster my desires are fulfilled, and the smoother and more peaceful my life becomes.

10. All things that I give, send out, share, or donate come back to me a hundredfold, and I am truly grateful.

11. Everything is running smoothly; all obstacles are removed.

12. In all matters, God will go before me and make the rugged places plain.

13. Everything works out in divine order. Everything falls miraculously into place. Negative people and situations are not around me.

14. God's desires and my desires are the same. I do not desire what I am not supposed to have or experience.

15. Everything gets better and better. There are no limits to my wholistic prosperity. God's treasures of health, happiness, and joy are endless.

16. The truth of every situation is always revealed to me.

By reviewing your personal holistic Future Plan scrapbook and affirmations every day, you can begin on the road to a brighter future. These affirmations are vital in the materialization of your hopes and dreams because they help you to move quickly to the pot of gold at the end of the rainbow. It is important to write down your goals and daily objectives, to increase their potency.

Here are some examples of short-term and long-term goals:

SHORT-TERM GOALS	LONG-TERM GOALS
1. I will have the dining room redecorated in my house by the end of one year.	1. I would like to have the work completed in six weeks.
2. I will create a positive affirmation list today and will affirm it over and over in the coming weeks.	2. I will attract the perfect mate.
3. I will lose eight pounds in the near future.	3. I will lose twenty-five pounds.
4. I will enroll in two courses this semester.	4. I will have my master's degree.
5. I will buy a new car this year.	5. I am saving $200 per month toward the down payment on a new car.

Goals and affirmations should be in your own words. You can assign a time frame to each desire, but remember that if it doesn't work out according to your time frame, it will work according to God's time frame. It *will be*—in *Divine Order.* Trust Him!

CREATIVE VISUALIZATION

There are several ways to supplement your personal holistic blueprint, making it even more effective in attracting good things to you. Much has been written about the powers of positive thinking, and rightly so. Positive thinking combined with creative visualization can take you to new planes of happiness and contentment you never before thought possible. The key to all this is learning to control your subconscious mind.

Metaphysicians and experts on positive thinking may express their philosophies in different words, but basically we all have discovered the same thing: Creative visualization is a powerful tool to use in shaping our lives. The techniques are consistent and very simple.

It has been said that "all things evolve out of consciousness." Nothing happens in your life that is not first recorded in your subconscious mind. This recording is done through the subconscious impressions of your feelings and ideas. Thus, in order to control the subconscious you must learn to control your feelings. Whenever you are depressed or hurting, those feelings are impressed on your subconscious and eventually manifest themselves as negative events in your life. On the other hand, if you could learn to feel only positive things about the situations that confront you, you could put the subconscious to work at bringing positive things your way.

Be careful and attentive of your moods and feelings at all times, as there is an unbroken connection between what you feel is happening in your life and what actually happens.

I know of a very good-looking man who doesn't monitor his thinking. He is moody, very sarcastic, complains frequently, and allows himself to become very unhappy. Yet he cannot see why his relationships never work out. He doesn't understand that it is his attitude that creates the difficulties and unhappiness and that by changing his thinking he could change his life.

Statistics prove that more than half of all diseases (some claim it is *all* diseases) are brought on by emotional disturbances impressed upon the subconscious. Strong guilt feelings or negative feelings of any kind seep into the very depths of your subconscious mind, doing their dirty work, very likely making you sick either physically, emotionally, or mentally.

Some people go through life thinking that chance or an accident is responsible for their maladies, or that their fate is predestined by the stars. Actually, what you impress on your subconscious mind, through your conscious mind, determines most of the conditions of your existence. Like an impersonal, nonselective machine, the subconscious simply *accepts* as real what you perceive to be real.

As for the stars, the most competent astrologers will tell you that the planets indicate *proclivities*, but that we still have free choice to determine how our lives will play out. Astrology, they say, is a *tool*.

While the belief that "you are what you think" can be a scary prospect, the point is to use this potentially limitless power for your own benefit. If your negative thoughts and feelings can wreak havoc on your life pattern, then so can positive feelings work for you, to make you the person you always wanted to be! This seems amazingly simple, but all you have to do is *try it*, to find out.

To start the creative visualization process working for you, you must first assume the feeling or mental state you would be in if you already had realized your wishes. It isn't necessary to think about *how* these objectives might be accomplished; just *feel* that you already are enjoying the fruits of your labor. *Know* it to be so.

If you dwell on the difficulties of attaining a particular goal, or even the seeming impossibility of it, you will be putting up barriers which will keep you from getting what you want. Dwelling on obstacles produces them. To feel a situation is hopeless or to consider yourself a failure will cause the subconscious to make failure a reality for you. *Be*, rather, *a success!*

Complete control of all your thoughts and feelings must be your ultimate goal. One way to avoid scattered thinking is to force yourself to become more organized and to practice following through on projects. It also is helpful to use the tools of sleep and prayer to help attain that state of mind you would be in if all your goals were met.

If you wish for a new boat, visualize yourself gliding across the water in it. Feel the salt spray on your face; enjoy the whole experience as though it were actually happening. If you want a certain person to be closer to you, think of being with him or her—and think of how happy it makes you both to be together.

Remember, the key to making the process work is the *feeling*. Besides the mental picture (the creative visualization), you must actually *feel* what it will be like when that visualization—your dream—comes true. *Positive statements alone, without feeling, will not reach deep enough to unleash the powers of your subconscious mind.* You must consciously *be* or *have* what you want, while you fall asleep. Never go to sleep feeling sad, angry, or disillusioned. Once you fall asleep, you lose control over the situation; your subconscious mind takes over, feeding on those thoughts your conscious mind was entertaining when you dropped off to sleep. *Never read anything disturbing or watch anything violent on television before retiring.*

Morning is another time when your mind is ripe for creative suggestion. Command to yourself the following ideals, or any others you choose:

LOVE: I send love to everyone I see. I accept the love that others throughout the universe are directing at me. Hate and resentment are not part of my life.

PEACE OF MIND: I am at perfect peace. All conflicts are removed from my being. Serenity flows throughout the universe and within me.

HEALTH: My mind, in connection with my body, demands all my organs to function properly. My mind is in perfect working order.

WEALTH: I accept the avalanches of wealth that are coming my way. I am aware that the universe provides all my necessities and much, much more!

Before any request or visualization can materialize, you must first have the desire to receive it. Desire opens the door for the forces to begin working with your higher self on these projects of the heart. Many people think desire is a destructive, negative emotion, but this is not so. Every healthy person has desires for a better life, more success in business, the love of another person, and other, individual things. Desire is a positive emotion; it is good for you. Learning to accept that fact will bring you only happiness, if you desire things that are not harmful to others.

The only condition attached to attaining your desires is that you must truly believe you will receive what you ask for. Nothing will be withheld from you if you really are sincere. The instant you accept your desires as fact, your subconscious mind begins to find ways to make them come true. *The mind is the most powerful tool known to man.*

It is important to understand that *action* and *effort* are a crucial part of this process, that visualization is not wishful thinking. You won't become a medical doctor just by visualizing yourself in that position.

Eventually, with practice, you will find your subconscious and conscious minds existing in the same reality. You will learn never to think negatively, for fear of bringing negativity into your life. You will know, instead, that to make every situation in your life positive, every desire attainable (with the accompanying action and effort), you need only to visualize it creatively.

In his fine book *The Power of Your Subconscious Mind*, Dr. Joseph Murphy says, "What, in your opinion, is the master secret of the ages? . . . The answer is extraordinarily simple. The secret is the marvelous, miracle-working power found in your own subconscious mind, the last place most people would seek it. You can bring into your life more power, more wealth, more health, more happiness, and more joy by learning to contact and release the hidden power of your subconscious mind. You need not acquire this power; you already possess it. But, you want to learn how to use it; you want to understand it so that you can apply it in all departments of your life. . . .

The Infinite Intelligence within your subconscious mind will reveal to you everything you need to know at every moment of time and point of space, provided you are open-minded and receptive."

I believe every word of this, and I practice it daily.

VISUALIZATION TECHNIQUES

Visualization helps to repel or neutralize negative energy by programming your conscious and subconscious mind to bring about the desired results. Through this process you can be free of the physical, mental, spiritual, and emotional chains that bind you.

There are many types of visualization techniques. You can make up your own. I have used three, in particular, which have proven to be especially effective, as each eliminates the negativity caused by a specific person or situation:

1. The Magic Mirror Technique
2. The Freezer Method
3. The Spacesuit Method

The Magic Mirror Technique is somewhat ritualistic in nature, but I believe it helps greatly to impress the subconscious mind. To use this method, place a small mirror on top of and facing a photo or picture of the person or situation disturbing you. If you use crystals, place a crystal on the back of the mirror to magnify the reflection. This method works by the "boomerang" effect: The negative deeds, plans, or thoughts will be reflected back to the person or situation generating them. You will often find out about it later and will discover this method does, indeed, work!

The Freezer Technique also repels negative energy. On a piece of paper, write the name of the person who is causing difficulties in your life. Wrap the paper in foil and place it in the freezer. Whatever the person tries to do to you will become frozen and will remain out of your life, frozen in any attempts to do anything more to you.

The Spacesuit Method is strictly a mental process and an equally effective technique. First, imagine in your mind that you are in a spacesuit of brilliant, protective, divine white light. Know that nothing of a negative nature can penetrate this spacesuit. Any negativity of any sort will automatically be repelled or neutralized. Now, feel refreshed and relieved. Keep "God's Spacesuit" around you at all times. See it in our mind. You will see how negative circumstances around you will begin to diminish, go away, or just not disturb you as much as before utilizing this wondrous technique. (Do you remember that President Reagan often was called "the Teflon president"? Perhaps he lives in just such a spacesuit! Certainly, he had an air of serenity about him.)

INTUITION

Intuition is "gut feeling"—knowing something without the use of rational processes. It is a natural ability in which you learn by suspending judgment and listening to your inner voice. Having a clear, quiet mind promotes the best intuitive state, so meditation is a powerful way to increase your intuition.

Why develop intuition? People who "just happen" to be at the right place at the right time, and for whom good things happen with uncanny frequency, are not just lucky. They have strong intuition. Truly successful executives are those who rely on their intuitive psychic abilities.

Intuition brings better decision making, more creative ideas, deeper insight, and more fulfillment. It provides options and alternatives as well as joy, wisdom, and inner peace. Accurate intuition helps us gain insight into ourselves, into other people, and into our environment. It also can lead to valuable predictions of the future.

According to Laurie Nadel, author of *Sixth Sense: The Whole-*

Brain Book of Intuition, Hunches, Gut Feelings, and Their Place in Everyday Life, intuition gives you the *whole* picture, not just the steps it takes to get there. Nadel notes that people who are very logical can only see things in steps, and therefore have a harder time being intuitive. Men, who often are not comfortable with the term "intuition" (perhaps because of the expression, "a *woman's* intuition"), may refer to a "hunch" or a "gut feeling," but they are all the same.

Paul Sawchenko, an associate professor at the Salk Institute for Biological Studies, La Jolla, California, says evidence suggests that intuition originates in the brain's right hemisphere. Researchers have found that women do, indeed, have a larger structure of nerve fibers linking the right and left hemispheres, which makes for faster response time in blending intuition and logic.

The corporate world has caught on to the benefits and now test for intuitive skills. Intuitive people are better at making quick, difficult decisions. Some believe this is why the Japanese, whose culture places great importance on intuition and spirituality, have advanced rapidly in technology and business.

PROGRAMMING TECHNIQUES FOR PROSPERITY

It has been said that you don't have to be a millionaire to be happy. Still, if you have only enough money to survive physically, you will spend all your time worrying about how to pay bills and eat. Such worrisome thoughts block out higher, creative thoughts and, in turn, contribute to your poor situation.

An insurance company study revealed an amazing fact: Out of 100 people of age twenty-five, by the time they reach sixty-five (retirement age), 57 will be broke, 37 will have died, 5 will be financially secure, and only one will be rich.

Financial prosperity is a key element in the achievement of a totally holistic life. God never intended you to live in poverty or even near-poverty. To have enough money to be comfortable in life is not a sin. In fact, it is in most ways very beneficial—to both the individual and to society.

Having lofty ideals and pursuing them with the conviction that they are absolutely attainable is a trait to be admired. In fact, you will find that to be characteristic of every successful person on earth. Set out to do your very best—to be the best at what you do—in whatever you do. Be willing to be a little bit different from the rest of the crowd. Focus on the top and eliminate that stumbling block between you and success: a self-limiting state of mind.

It is important to have a plan to attain your goals and a time frame in which to accomplish them. Doing this will not only help to program your mind for the attainment of the goals, it will also show your persistence, organization, vision, and faith.

You must learn to enjoy everything you do, whether it is washing the dishes, pulling weeds, finishing a report, or doing a task not of your own choosing. A positive attitude makes you feel better and helps to relieve the stress otherwise caused by dissatisfaction. Wasting time being unhappy is something you can choose to do—or not to do. You have the option to make the best of a situation by thinking of positive things, meditating, or even making a game of it. You have it in your power to turn lemons into lemonade.

Picture in your mind what you realistically want, and believe it will be yours. Use your imagination to visualize in detail your financial desires.

In his book *You, Too, Can Be Prosperous*, Robert A. Russell reminds us that positive thoughts can:

- improve your finances
- strengthen your faith
- build your character
- attract opportunities
- abort disasters
- increase business
- neutralize negative emotions (fear, worry, sorrow, grief)
- heal disease

- stimulate the mind
- increase creativity
- dispel fear
- reverse negative situations
- create peace
- eliminate debts
- expand the mind
- elevate the consciousness
- quickly solve problems
- deter or eliminate hardships

Russell suggests an excellent affirmation to accomplish these goals. It is, very simply, "I am Prosperity." The following, from his book, clearly illustrates the impact of this affirmation:

It must be backed up with our earnest faith and desire. Your idea of prosperity may be a better position, more income, a nice vacation, an agreeable companion, or more health. It may be something you do not have but need desperately. The Law says you can have anything you desire, if you believe you already have it. That is, if you have a subjective acceptance of the thing desired. Now, contemplate that for a few moments. Not the money to meet the mortgage, not the new car, not the new house, but THE BASIC IDEA: 'I AM PROSPERITY!' Seek ye first the kingdom of God and everything shall be added unto you.

We must strive to achieve God consciousness as our source of an unlimited abundance of answers to our earthly problems. When you change your consciousness, you change the world.

Russell further explains prosperity and our ability to attract it:

We all want wealth in one form or another. Our financial wealth comes not through special abilities, talents, thrift, influence, environment, favorable conditions, or physical effort. It comes as a result of thinking, acting, and believing in a certain way. Those who follow this way, consciously or unconsciously, purposefully or accidentally, get definite results. Those who do not follow this way remain in want.

It is not a matter of choosing a particular locality, line of activity, business, profession, or job. It is not a matter of living in Podunk, Iceland, or Florida. It is not a matter of being bright or dull, smart or stupid, strong or weak, sickly or well. It is a matter of doing things in a certain way and of holding to that way through thick or thin. The potentiality of one is the potentiality of all. If anybody has wealth, you can have wealth; if anybody has a beautiful home, you can have a beautiful home.

The Law of Supply is no respecter of persons. Since like produces like, and since the Law of Cause and Effect works in the same way for all persons at all times, anybody who follows the Law will infallibly demonstrate an abundant supply.

In other words, expect more from yourself and don't concentrate so much on competition and/or dependence on others.

Remember, you are unique, unlike any other person in the universe. Not only must you be yourself, you also have to believe in yourself, in order to succeed in any endeavor you choose. *A positive self-image is vital!*

Though you are unique, everything in the universe is interconnected. You are not a loose part, but a link in a chain. As such, you must strive to maintain harmony with your fellow man. Visualize yourself growing richer and richer every day; see yourself prospering and others prospering with you. Never wish a bad circumstance on another person, because that wish will return to you. In fact, bless everything you give or send out. Even bless the bills you send out! Remember that, if given with a good attitude, everything you give will result in more returning. It is· "bread cast upon the waters."

Before you ask the universe for the prosperity you desire, know where you want to go in life. Have an ultimate dream, a goal, in mind, and be willing to work for it. Always continue learning, as exploring new sources will help you to achieve all your goals in a shorter amount of time. Then, and only then, ask the universe, the superconscious mind, to reveal money-making ideas to your conscious mind. Set time aside, daily, for this request. Remember that the superconscious mind is the Divine Mind, the God-force within, the Creative Intelligence, and the Intuitive Mind. It is *this* force that reveals information to your subconscious and, ultimately, to your conscious mind.

Once you have placed this request of the God-force within you, in your superconscious mind, you will be able to move on to the subconscious mind. Learning to control your subconscious mind can also bring you great prosperity.

Having mastered the positive-thinking techniques, you will be ready to try these self-programming exercises:

1. Begin by sitting quietly and comfortably in a peaceful place. Take a few deep breaths to relax, slowly counting to five as you inhale, and exhaling to the count of ten. Deep breathing charges your mind and body with electromagnetic energy. If there are problems in any area of your life, ask the Higher Intelligence within for the answers. Acknowledge that you are grateful for even the difficulties life brings, knowing there is a purpose for everything and that hard times are learning experiences, too. These

thoughts open up a channel of answers, guidance,
and positive changes

2. Have trust and faith in this Higher Intelligence by
preparing yourself for the changes you are imagin-
ing in your creative visualization. If you want to be
a pilot, enroll in a flying course. If you want to
travel, get out your suitcase, dust it off, and put
a toothbrush in it. If you want a date for the
weekend, buy an outfit you would wear for it.
Prepare yourself as though your aspirations already have come true. In doing so, you are proving your faith.

3. Affirmations are valuable tools for achieving financial freedom. Use these, or make up your own:

"God is my unfailing supply, and abundance in all forms
comes to me quickly, under His grace and perfect ways.
Only that which is true of the Father is true for me, for I
and the Father are one. As I am one with God, I am one
with good, for God is both the giver and the gift."

4. Prayer is an important programming technique
underestimated by those who have lost hope when
their prayers were not immediately answered. But
there is a way to pray which brings results. Remember that God works in mysterious but deliberate
ways. We have created many of our problems by
eating poorly, not controlling our thoughts and
emotions, or by succumbing to whims and indiscriminate indulgences. You should always first praise
God for everything in your life and then ask for bad
circumstances to be healed or released, so that bet-

ter things will replace them. Prayer, like creative visualization, is based on complete faith. According to Mark 11:24, "What things soever ye desire, when ye pray believe that ye receive them, and ye shall have them." The importance of prayer cannot be overemphasized as a tool for a successful life. God is like a cosmic computer: By using the tools of prayer, positive programming, and meditation, you "program" the universal "computer" to provide for all your needs. Of course, to be blessed with God's help you must follow His laws, the basis of which is love. Prayers against others and harmful thought-programming will only reflect negatively on you. Always remember that what you send out comes back.

5. Finally, be patient. Go about your business and don't worry about how everything is going to materialize. It all will be arranged cosmically. In fact, you may even get better results than you requested.

To attract prosperity you must do your homework. Every day, visualize exactly what you need. Don't let negative thoughts from yourself or others interfere with your belief that your wishes will come true. It is best not to share your goals with individuals who are not attuned to you.

These techniques represent not *wishful* thinking but, rather, *positive* thinking. And they work!

NEGATIVE THOUGHT

Making negative comments like, "I can't" or "I won't" or "I'm not" tears down the positive thought forms you've spent so much time building. Remember that, if you *say* you can't, you *can't*, because that's what you have placed in your subconscious. Negative words and thoughts can destroy everything you've worked for. As thought creators, we have an obligation to make sure we never use this power in a negative way. Research already has proven that, wrongly stimulated, our thoughts can produce the symptoms of any disease, can cause mental illness, and can cause harm to others. The negative use of mental energy can also manifest through such things as voodoo, "black magic" and witchcraft.

Rightly stimulated, our thoughts can give us peace of mind, happiness, health, and long life. *We make the choices that affect our world.* I believe that "bad luck" is a direct result of distorted thinking. By thinking dark, negative thoughts, you jeopardize your own future, since these thoughts cause negative things to happen in your life. Belief and the power of suggestion program the mind and influence your existence.

We cannot avoid thinking, but we can learn to make our thoughts more orderly, more direct, and more well-meaning. Controlling your mind in a healthy, positive way will help you avoid falling victim to the negative thinkers around you. Surround yourself with others who think positively, about you and about themselves, who have high goals in life, and who are in control of their thoughts. The effect of this synergy will be more effective thought power. As you begin to use the techniques for positive thinking, you will attract this sort of desirable person to you.

PRACTICAL METAPHYSICS

All the positive thinking in the world won't do any good unless you back it up with positive action. We are in a constant battle to change the limitations placed on our lives by physical imperfections, our material environment, and random events beyond our control, and we need all the positive elements possible going for us, to prevail in this challenge. That includes going out and physically working for the desired ends.

God rewards hard workers, not people who only dream and expect. Fulfillment of your desires requires that you take full advantage of opportunities that appear as a result of positive thinking, but *positive thinking must always be accompanied by positive, hard work.*

Many people wonder why they cannot immediately have exactly what they want. What they don't realize is that, *to attain goals, you must be dedicated to them and willing to work for them.* This sometimes requires great sacrifice. Some people are not willing to change their lives on all levels; others cling to bad habits or unfruitful relationships. If you don't follow a completely holistic lifestyle, with attention to spiritual, physical, and mental principles, it is likely you will not be successful at achieving all you desire. *Your percentage of success is directly proportional to your percentage of dedication.* The person who chooses to strive for perfection holistically is taking the most direct route to happiness. It takes a lot of work and discipline, but it results in an enjoyable, fulfilling, and healthy way of life.

THE UNIVERSAL LAWS

From the multitude of people I have counseled in a wide range of matters, I have gleaned some interesting data on and insight into human desires. Almost all seek the same things: health, wealth, ideal companionship, peace of mind, spiritual bliss, an ideal working environment, and a perfect home life. No one wants to be lonely, sick, or poor; no one wants to waste time, energy, or money. All want the divine blessings, all the riches of the universe, but—with few exceptions—none know how to go about getting them.

To obtain the desired blessings and riches, in our lives, we must first understand and apply what are known as the Universal Laws. These laws are operative whether or not you know about them; ignorance of them (as with local, state, and national laws) is no excuse. If you are not getting what you want in life, it could be that you are unaware of or have been ignoring one or more of these laws.

Think of the Universal Laws as numbers on a combination lock: Each number is an integral part of the combination, necessary to open the lock successfully. The complete combination of laws will open the door to your total, holistic happiness.

Although there are great numbers of them, I consider the following thirty-one (in alphabetical order) to be most important in achieving a holistic life:

1. The Law of Abundance
2. The Law of Balance and Harmony
3. The Law of Cause and Effect (The Law of Karma)
4. The Law of Command
5. The Law of Compassion
6. The Law of Consideration
7. The Law of Cycles
8. The Law of Desire
9. The Law of Dynamic Action
10. The Law of Evolution
11. The Law of Faith
12. The Law of Forgiveness
13. The Law of Free Will and Predestination
14. The Law of Healing
15. The Law of Hygienic Living
16. The Law of Increase
17. The Law of Love and Goodwill
18. The Law of Loyalty and Integrity
19. The Law of Magnetic Attraction
20. The Law of Mental Imaging
21. The Law of Order
22. The Law of Persistence
23. The Law of Praise
24. The Law of Prayer
25. The Law of Productivity
26. The Law of Release
27. The Law of Substitution
28. The Law of Thrift and Conservation
29. The Law of Transmutation
30. The Vacuum Law of Prosperity (The Law of Release)
31. The Law of Vision

The application of these divine universal laws governs our physical, mental, emotional, and spiritual state of being. The failure to apply them will result in fewer positive returns. Broken laws mean a buildup of bad karma that eventually will have to be paid for. Properly applied, the laws will consistently solve your problems and will become the foundation for a happy and fulfilled life.

Primary among the laws—those to which you should pay closest and greatest attention—are the Law of Praise, the Law of Cause and Effect (Karma), the Law of Mental Imaging, the Law of Prayer, and the Vacuum Law of Prosperity. But remember that each and every one of the thirty-one laws listed above is at work in determining the quality of your life. Read carefully the following explanations of the laws and consider how best to integrate them into your everyday existence.

1. *The Law of Abundance.* This law is based on the importance of living in attunement with God. To have abundance is your divine birthright. If you regularly attune yourself to God, the Creative Intelligence—by keeping faith and expectation—He will supply all your needs and you will have an abundant life.

Jane prided herself on her self-reliance and her rejection of all things spiritual in her life. A fast-track yuppie, she had no time to think of anything other than making vice president of her company and collecting her fair share of "toys" along the way. Suddenly, with the death of her mentor, the ground seemed to fall away beneath her feet, and the whole world seemed empty of purpose. A close friend from Jane's childhood, who had watched with dismay as Jane dropped all her old companions, convinced the frantic yuppie that God would help her if only she would ask. It was neither easy nor quick, but after months of patient discussion, reading, and praying, Jane developed a relationship with God and saw her whole world change. She continued to be successful in her job, but found new enjoyment and meaning in it. She rediscovered some of her "best friends" from her youth and found new friends with whom she had more in common than the desire to make as much money as fast as possible. Her relationship with God continues to grow, as does the abundance in her life.

2. *The Law of Balance and Harmony.* All things are designed on a supreme universal scale of balance and harmony that creates order. When something happens to upset this delicate system of natural order, a reciprocal or reactive event always takes place. For example, when the body needs rest or is lacking some nutrient, it goes out of balance and becomes a prime target for disease.

Keep every aspect of your life in balance and harmony. A part of your day should be devoted to mental relaxation, another part for introspection, another for loved ones, work, physical activity, etc. If you spend too much time on any one aspect, the others will suffer— which ultimately means that you will suffer. An unbalanced life leads to disharmony. A working mother, for example, must balance work, home, husband, and children. But if she does not plan time for herself, then her health, happiness, and relationships all will suffer.

This law is really the balance wheel of the cosmos. Without balance and harmony, the universe would consist only of chaos and catastrophe. You cannot break this law without breaking yourself, thereby causing ill health and unhappiness.

Rabbi Sol Landau, founder of the MidLife Services Foundation, in Miami, feels that midlife crises often are caused by a lack of balance. One man he describes told the rabbi, "I'm making more money than I ever dreamed was possible. Why am I so unhappy?" It turned out the man had spent so much time making money, he had neglected his family, his friends, and his health. A philanthropist of some note, he still felt "unconnected" to many of the causes he supported. Once he realized that by balancing his life better he could "stop to smell the flowers," he turned over a large part of his business responsibility to his daughter, discovered how much he enjoyed his grandchildren, began walking and talking with his wife, and became a warmer, happier person than he had ever been before. He also joined the board of his favorite charity and became involved in a much more personal and fulfilling way. *Balance* was the key.

3. *The Law of Cause and Effect.* This law can also be called the Law of Karma, Divine Retribution, Giving and Receiving, or Compensation. It means that you get out of life whatever you put into it. You reap what you sow.

Karma is a concept basic to Hinduism and Buddhism. It says that one's state in this life is the result of physical and mental actions in past incarnations, and that what you do in this life can determine your destiny in future incarnations. Ignorance of the Law of Karma will not exempt you from being affected by it. Your words and deeds count in all you do.

All of life is a learning process. Each experience is a result of what came before it. We are put on this earth to learn the lessons we had not learned before, and if we continue to ignore the consequences of our actions, we will simply have to repeat those lessons until we get them right.

A woman who came to me for counseling complained that she always seemed to attract men who drank too much. She herself hardly drank at all, so it was not a matter of meeting men in bars. In addition, she had what she described as a "Florence Nightingale Complex"—constantly finding herself in the position of "nursing" the men in her life. A past-life regression showed she had treated alcoholics quite harshly; she was obviously here to learn to be more compassionate toward this group of people. I explained to her that she could accomplish this by volunteering in a clinic or helping the homeless, many of whom are alcoholics, rather than attracting them as dates or mates.

There is no way to determine when or how a person will pay for misdeeds, but it is certain that he or she will pay. (The positive or negative *karma*, or payment from the sum total, is not always immediately evident.) Think carefully about what you say and do. Pray for guidance, and know that what you put out into the universe will come back to you. It is not your place to retaliate or to seek vengeance on another person: The universe will take notice and will hold all accountable for their actions. The only thing you should do is send thoughts of love and forgiveness.

4. *The Law of Command.* Through this law, you cause to happen all the things you have been programming in your holistic Future Plan and scrapbook of destiny. Always assert positively that everything you want from life is yours. This produces a feeling of control that will send out the vibrations necessary to help you achieve those things. Never have the attitude that you *wish* something would happen: The word *wish* usually implies something unattainable. Instead, take control of the situation and *affirm* that it has or will definitely happen. Be careful, here, as your subconscious mind will take your comments as a command.

A client came to me for a nutritional consultation. She was having shoulder and neck pains that occurred only when she was at work. She wondered whether the pains might be diet related, but after a lengthy discussion, I learned that she couldn't stand her job and frequently commented that it was "a pain in the neck." I suggested that she refrain from making comments of that sort, explaining that she was negatively programming her mind. Within a week the pain had subsided, and by three weeks they were gone completely. This is an example of how very great the power of command is.

5. *The Law of Compassion.* Always feel empathy with others, extending a helping hand to those in need, and seek ways to comfort others, out of kindness and compassion.

Stephanie, a teenager, was brought to me by her mother, who was—rightfully—concerned that her daughter seemed to be losing all her friends. Rather than being upset about it, Stephanie felt the fault lay only with the other girls and boys in her crowd and said she didn't really care. She couldn't understand why her mother was so upset; she could always find other friends who would appreciate her sense of humor. It turned out this "sense of humor" had a cruel streak associated with it. In fact, most of her old friends didn't find her brand of humor funny at all: She was constantly making fun of the poor, the weak, the less attractive, and the less intelligent. When she mimicked the walk of a girl on crutches, it was the last straw. Her friends just dropped her, wanting nothing more to do with her. We spent a good deal of time together, examining why Stephanie behaved as she did. When, one day, she broke down in tears, I knew I had gotten through to her. She resolved to change her ways and to show herself and her old friends she could be a person of kindness and compassion. She began by volunteering at the hospital for crippled children and found herself going out of her way to help those less fortunate. At last report, Stephanie had won the admiration of students, teachers, and the hospital administration, and was on her way to a very productive and exemplary life.

6. *The Law of Consideration.* Respect the feelings, personal space, and will of others. This includes respecting others' thoughts, words, and deeds. Take time to show others you care. This law is closely tied to the Golden Rule: "Do unto others as you would have them do unto you."

A great many marriages fail because the partners lack an understanding of the importance of this Law. Especially in an era when many who marry have had independent lives of their own for some time, it is crucial that neither spouse feel "smothered" by the other. I recall an older man (married forty years) telling me, "I love my wife dearly, but if I didn't know that once each year I could get away and go hunting with my buddies, I don't think I could have stayed married." Both men and women need to know that certain space in their home is for them alone. When a man spreads his things all over every room in the house, leaving no table or desk top free for his wife, it indicates his lack of respect for her and her needs. Conversely, if the bathroom cabinet is so full of makeup and perfume that there is no space for shaving cream, the wife lacks respect for her husband's needs.

Conversation should not be a spawning ground for arguments, and it won't be if each of the conversants shows respect for the other's opinion. There are ways of disagreeing without making the other person feel belittled. In a tribute to the departing Consul-General of Israel, Dr. Moshe Liba, the editor of the *Miami Herald* commented: "Dr. Liba could disagree vehemently with you without making you feel he was thinking 'and besides that, you're stupid.' "

Debaters learn this at the beginning of their training. It would benefit us all to keep this Law in mind.

7. *The Law of Cycles.* Author Vera Stanley Alder, in *The Finding of the Third Eye,* says of the universe, "The same system of form, time, and motion runs through the whole universe, so that if we properly study an atom or cell we will obtain the key to the workings of a man, planet, or constellation. . . . There is an ordered arrangement within the universe, with certain periods of time and patterns of forms repeated up the scale and governing the tiniest to the greatest." Her description of the universe coincides with the principle that everything in the material world operates in cycles. This includes man and animal, plants, even inanimate objects.

Everything in nature has a distinct beginning and ending and, in between, a particular pattern, or rhythm, of existence. If we learn to recognize these high and low cycles, we can better take advantage of opportunities that come our way.

Think of all the aspects of your life: health, relationships, business dealings, etc. If you analyzed each of them, plotting their highs and lows as individual curves on a graph, you would find they have a definite cyclical pattern. This is a simplified explanation of the Law of Cycles, but it helps to explain why sometimes everything is going your way and then, suddenly, when you enter a low cycle in one of those areas, things begin to go wrong. You may be in a high cycle in one aspect of your life while another aspect is going through a low cycle.

External events can trigger a low cycle. Your moods also affect cycles, and your general holistic health is closely connected to whether you are high or low at a particular time. *You have control over your life cycles.* They are *not* inevitable cycles in which you helplessly ride up and down. If you sense a low health cycle coming on, for instance, be more careful about what you eat, and get plenty of rest. That may be enough to stop the cycle before you become ill.

As you become more aware of your psychic abilities and intuition, you will also be more aware of these life cycles, how to recognize and deal with them.

8. *The Law of Desire.* All progress and fulfillment begins with the seed of desire. Make a written list of your desires, recognizing that they are necessary and admirable in achieving your life's goals. Put down as many as you want, and use creative visualization techniques to make them come true. Make sure your desires are of a positive nature and are not intended to hurt anyone.

One of the most revealing answers, in a discussion of complaints, comes in response to the question, "Did you *tell* him (her) what it was you wanted?" As you may have guessed, the answer usually is "No," following a rather quizzical look. It simply does not occur to many of us to express our wishes and desires clearly. Somehow, we have assimilated the lesson that *asking* for things is not nice. In fact, nothing could be further from the truth: How can you get *anywhere* if you don't know *where* you want to go? This is the philosophy behind all the Customer Service departments in major stores and companies. Realizing they lost business because unhappy customers said nothing but took their business elsewhere, companies now offer the opportunity for you to tell them what you want. In considering your life's goals, think deeply and state them clearly and positively. "*Wishing* won't make it so," but action based on concrete *desire* will.

9. *The Law of Dynamic Action.* Taking the first step and then following through is what dynamic action is all about. Application of this law activates the entire being, keeping us holistically young, vital, and energetic. This law is particularly useful when you are confronted with difficult experiences, as the first step often is the most challenging.

Just as the writer who suffers a block when confronted by a blank page sees his words flow once he has written the first sentence, so you will conquer your difficulties, fearlessly and spiritually, through dynamic action, and you will become stronger mentally and physically.

Do not allow a fear of failure to prevent you from taking that first step. In a study of Americans who had made $1 million before the age of thirty, it was found that each of them had gone bankrupt at least once. That reality may be too harsh for most of us to accept, but it illustrates the importance of getting out there and making a move. Think about the times you hesitated to go swimming, thinking the water too cold. Putting your toe in confirms your fear, but if you take the plunge and jump or dive in, you discover the water is warmer below the surface. Once in the water, you find yourself refreshed and wondering why you didn't go in sooner. Dynamic Action is one of the keys to successful, holistic life.

10. *The Law of Evolution.* This law assures that our soul will eventually progress to become one with God. If you are going

through hard times, it does not mean you are going backward. An evolutionary process is still going on. Learning by experience is evolutionary; it is by learning that we progress.

A child I know, whom I believe to be "an old soul," is a keen observer of people and life in general. One evening, seeing his mother distraught by the number of things that had gone wrong that day, he approached her and asked, Mommy, why do you get so upset and angry when things go wrong? Each time you do something the wrong way, you learn to do it differently the next time. Think how much you are learning!" What wisdom there is in that child's comment. It is said that, in the Chinese language, there is no word for "problem," only one for "opportunity." Since I do not speak Chinese, I don't know whether or not that's true, but the theory behind it conforms to the Law of Evolution.

11. *The Law of Faith. Believe* in the fulfillment of your desires, and they will be fulfilled. Refrain from using negative statements such as, "I am afraid," or "I don't think I can make it," or "I am worried about the future." Statements of that kind counteract the metaphysical power that works through your subconscious mind to bring about your desires. Faith is the power of positive thinking.

In the highest sense, faith refers to a belief in the Universal Intelligence (God), an understanding and acceptance that each person must establish for himself. It consists of a *knowing* trust, attained through personal spiritual experience. As the Bible says, "If you have faith as small as a mustard seed, you can say to this mountain, 'Move from here to there,' and it will move. Nothing will be impossible for you" (Matthew 17:20).

A friend of mine made extra money tutoring those who had difficulty passing the math section of the Florida Real Estate Exam. When asked how many lessons would be necessary, she always shocked her prospective students by telling them they would learn all the math in one two-hour session. Told she was underestimating the difficulty, as these were hard-core mathematical illiterates, she explained, "The reason you have not been able to do the math is that you haven't understood the explanations. I'm going to show you an easy way to approach the problems, and you'll see you'll 'get it' immediately. After that, it's just a question of practice, and I'll give you lots of samples to take home with you. I've never yet had anyone fail." My friend's students—all adults—approached their tutoring sessions with new faith and belief in themselves, and—just as she had promised—every one of them passed the math on the next try.

12. *The Law of Forgiveness.* Prophets and spiritual teachers throughout the ages have taught us to forgive our fellow man, which is often easier said than done. But in order to neutralize any negativity directed toward us, we must master the Law of Forgiveness. If we don't forgive, we allow the negative energy of the circumstance to "eat away" at us, and we consequently suffer in all aspects of our life.

You are accountable for your actions. If you send negative, you get negative; if you send positive and forgiving thoughts, you get positive thoughts and circumstances back. By sending out forgiving thoughts to someone who has hurt you, you cancel the negativity that otherwise would continue to recycle between you. Forgiving those who have deliberately hurt you may be a difficult task, but it is an important prerequisite to personal, emotional, and spiritual growth.

Remember to forgive yourself for any negative deeds for which you are sincerely sorry, and—in addition—ask God for forgiveness. Then, let the guilt and remorse go, for if you continue to dwell on those negative emotions produced by your thoughts, deeds, or words, it will block the good you wish to bring into your life.

One of the most touching stories I've heard came from a woman who had been estranged from her daughter, following a rather nasty divorce from the girl's father. For years the mother couldn't forgive either of them for the hurts and injustices she had suffered. Learning of the Law of Forgiveness and deciding to put it to use, the woman was amazed when, two days later, her daughter called to invite her to dinner for the first time. They both decided to forgive the past, and their relationship continues to grow in a positive direction.

13. *The Law of Free Will and Predestination.* Free will governs you, enabling you to make your own choices at all times. Even if you feel influenced by what you perceive as your destiny, you still have, even to the last moment, the option of free will. But predestination also plays a part in your life. The Divine Will, your higher self, has laid out a path for you to follow, if you so choose. In following this path, remember that all of us are moving toward the same ultimate purpose: to become more God-like. If you wonder what part of your life is predetermined, by "Fate," the answer is that you determine your own life by your daily thinking.

Even those like Billy Graham and Mother Teresa, who seem driven by a divine mission, actually have planned their own future. The higher self of each spiritual leader placed into his or her mind the idea to follow a particular path, but it was through effort and being attuned to this higher self that each of them came to have what appears to be a divinely ordained future.

The higher self is that spark of divinity in each of us. Spiritual leaders' will is God's will because they are so closely tied to it. But there also are plenty of people who do good work and don't attribute it to God's will. They simply have an inner drive to accomplish whatever personal mission they have. This inner drive, too, comes from the higher self. Thus, even an atheist can have a "divine mission" without realizing it or calling it that. It all ties in with the Law of Balance and Harmony, as some of your choices are in line with God's will and others are from your own free will. The amount of each depends upon your attunement to God.

Psychics, astrologers, and others who can accurately tune in to another person's future and make predictions about it are picking up on the predetermined circumstances ahead which have been "destined" by that person's continued daily thoughts. Those predictions will be borne out unless the individual completely and continually changes his or her thinking, thereby altering his or her destiny. You *create your own future* by choosing other thoughts and making other decisions. In addition, there are always risks on this planet—unexpected accidents or tragedies beyond our control. Between free will and risk, then, not all of a person's life is predetermined. Even if it were, no one has the ability to "see" it all beforehand.

In becoming aware of your purpose and living it, you will learn to express God's will in your life. If you choose to ignore it, you will learn to express it on the next spiritual plane.

Frequently, those who visit psychics and astrologers for guidance come with the impression that the details of their lives have been "cast in stone." But as Iris Saltzman, the renowned psychic astrologer, quotes to all who attend her sessions and classes in Miami, "The fool *obeys* the planets; the wise man *heeds* them." Each of us was born with certain *proclivities,* but it remains within our power to determine the exact course of our life, through our thoughts and actions.

14. *The Law of Healing.* Everyone has healing energy. This energy is an electromagnetic field that lies within and around your body. From the divine power source we can mentally direct this healing energy into our own body, mind, and spirit, or into those of others we wish to heal. This is explained more fully in other chapters of this book, but let me give you one example, here. A young boy who had been in a car crash in Texas was not expected to live, as a result of serious internal injuries. His aunt, hearing of the accident, gathered a group of spiritual friends at her home in North Carolina and,

together, they focused healing energy on the young boy—moving slowly from one part of his body to the next. They repeated this healing exercise twice a day. Within a week, the boy's mother had phoned her sister to say her son was making "a remarkable recovery" and that the doctors were "astounded." Something other than medical knowledge seemed to be at work, they said, but they couldn't explain it. It was the Law of Healing at work.

15. *The Law of Hygienic Living.* This law governs the needs of our physical bodies. We should strive to incorporate into our lives the following necessary health practices: breathing fresh, clean air; drinking pure water; following an oral hygiene program; eating a balanced, nutritious diet; getting proper rest and relaxation; and exercising regularly. All these practices are vital to making our physical body a worthy temple in which the God-force can dwell.

The Head Start program was designed, in part, to provide a nutritious breakfast for inner-city children who were coming to school with empty stomachs. If a child is hungry or malnourished, his brain cells will lack the nutrients to function properly. Long ago, it was discovered that many children diagnosed as hyperactive actually had an allergy to the sugars and preservatives that laced most of their food. More recently, in a breakthrough book, *Victory Over Diabetes*, a group of doctors has demonstrated that many of the wild swings in blood sugar levels of diabetics actually represent reactions not just to certain foods, but to environmental factors as well. Even among the offending foods, grains, dairy products, and beef were the culprits as often as simple sugars. Considering the severity of complications suffered by many diabetics, close attention to the Law of Hygienic Living should be a "given" to all who deal with such and similar illnesses. It was the Roman philosopher Seneca whose motto was, "A sound mind in a sound body." That serves us well, even twenty-three centuries later.

16. *The Law of Increase*. To ensure an increase in our holistic riches we must maintain an attitude of rich increase toward others. We lay this foundation by proving to the Creator that we are worthy to receive better things by taking care of what we already have. This will open the way to greater prosperity. Destructive criticism and condemnation subtract from that potential. So, if you see someone driving around town in a Rolls-Royce or Excalibur, don't envy him. Bless him instead, knowing that as you bless *his* prosperity you will attract prosperity to your own life.

Another writer I know told me of a phone call from a close friend, who had heard a report on television that the paperback rights to a book which already had been translated into eight languages were just sold for $2 million. The implication was that no one should be paid that kind of money for a book. My friend, rather than show envy or disgust, told the caller, "I think it's wonderful that woman's book has reached so many people all over the world. I hope mine will do the same." Undoubtedly, it will, as my friend—in blessing the other woman's prosperity—has helped to ensure her own.

17. *The Law of Love and Goodwill*. Love is the most powerful balancing and harmonizing force in the universe and should therefore be the basis for all our actions. Love can be personal and specific (consideration, affection, tenderness, devotion, loyalty) or impersonal and general (goodwill, understanding, helpfulness, cooperation, congeniality). In its purest form it is God's love for us and our love for God. You can deliberately produce divine love by thinking loving thoughts about others as well as about yourself.

As you regularly send love to all areas of your life, it is vitally important to send love to your problems, your debts, your ill health, etc. Radiating love to those who are negative, mean, or selfish is of utmost importance as well, because those are the people who most surely need it.

If a drunken driver hits your car, totally destroying it, but you narrowly escape with your life, sincerely send love and praise to the person who caused the accident. The spiritual love you send him may make him feel remorseful, may help him to quit drinking, or may help you get over the bitterness. It could, in fact, do any number of things to help improve the situation. This law, combined with the Law of Praise, will pave the quickest path to the realization of your goals, the solving of your problems, and the accomplishment of all you want in life. While all the universal laws form an integral part of achieving holistic happiness, these two laws are probably the most powerful among them.

Love is an unequaled power that brings with it the unification of the whole universe. As the Bible tells us, "There are three things that remain—faith, hope, and love—and the greatest of these is love" (Corinthians 13:13).

18. *The Law of Loyalty and Integrity.* Integrity is a positive, honest standard of values. Live your life with sincerity and straightforwardness. To be loyal to your efforts you must be loyal to yourself. One of Shakespeare's most quoted lines is, "This above all: to thine own self be true." Living that advice will give you a greater sense of well being. And, combining this law with the Law of Karma, the loyalty you give will be returned to you by others.

It has been extremely disturbing to read of the vast numbers of people participating in the decades of greed—which, we now know, do not belong to any one political party or segment of the population. Over and over again, I hear the lament, "Who are the role models? Not the politicians; not the businessmen; not the educators; not the clergy; not the sports figures." Integrity is seen, particularly by the young, as an "old-fashioned value," one which has no meaning or connection to their lives. In an era when situational ethics are considered the norm ("What's right for you may be wrong for me, so there *is* no 'right' or 'wrong' ") and it is considered by the most radical educators that teaching ethics in the schools is "an insult to the child's autonomy," it's no wonder so many people feel lost and disconnected from their fellow man and woman. Integrity is of the *utmost* importance, in our lives, and the earlier that lesson is taught, the sooner we will progress and evolve into truly holistic beings.

The mother of an eleven-year-old girl told me of finding a wallet with $150 but no identification, while vacationing in New Zealand. The young girl thought they should keep the money, feeling very lucky to have found it, but her mother asked how *she* would feel if she lost all *her* vacation money. As they drove to the nearest police station to leave the wallet, the young girl told her mother, "I think we should get a reward for turning it in." "That would be nice," her mother replied, "but if we don't, at least we'll know we did the right thing." Today, eighteen years later, the daughter remembers the incident with pride, as she raises her own children to lead lives of integrity.

19. *The Law of Magnetic Attraction.* Plant in your mental garden the seeds of the things you wish to attract. A seed in the soil is able to attract to itself the moisture and nourishment needed to fulfill its own predestined pattern. Just like planting seeds in the soil, you plant your mental picture in your subconscious mind. Form distinct mental pictures of the things you want, and through this law you will attract the desired conditions, opportunities, and people.

This law has nothing to do with physical science or magnets in which opposite poles attract. Rather, it is closer to the old saying, "Like attracts like." The person you are seeking very likely is seeking you with equal intensity. Many people say they are looking for "the perfect mate." This usually means someone who is intelligent, good-looking, financially stable, well organized, etc. But surprisingly few of these people possess the qualities they wish to attract! Having those qualities is an absolute necessity, not just to attract them but to maintain the relationship.

A man came to me last year, complaining that women seemed to find him attractive at first but that, after a few dates, always made excuses so as not to see him again. He was quick to explain that he knew just what he was looking for in a woman and, in fact, had met a number "with good potential" since he had come to town. After going over his list of necessary qualities, I turned the tables and asked about his own personality and lifestyle. He seemed quite surprised that he should be expected to *give* what he hoped to *receive*. He simply had never thought of relationships as "a two-way street." It follows the adage, "To *have* a friend, *be* a friend." What you *are* is what you will attract.

20. *The Law of Mental Imaging.* This is one of the most exciting concepts you can master, as you will learn that *you can create anything you can imagine.* Athletes and students throughout the world improve their performance through "visualization," the techniques of which are simple to explain and take only practice and confidence to acquire.

The mind has magical powers. It creates the pictures and plans which you turn into reality. Thinking is believing. You can produce whatever results you desire. But remember that this powerful mind can create both positive and negative images. You are constantly creating your life by the thoughts focused in your mind and imagination.

Remember *The Little Engine That Could?* He was far too small to climb that mountain (so everyone thought), but he kept saying, "I think I can! I think I can!" and—lo and behold!—he did!

The quarterback of the nation's top-ranked football team, preparing for the championship game, was asked what he did to get

himself ready. He explained that he practiced visualization techniques every day of the year and especially just before he went to
sleep at night—*seeing* himself handling the ball, throwing for touch-
downs, and winning the championship. His outstanding results, in
spite of his not having been considered the nation's best quarterback, are proof of the effectiveness of these exercises.

Another of my favorite examples is the result of a study done
on mediocre schoolchildren in Pennsylvania. They were divided
into two groups, with one set of students taught mental imaging.
(There are, by now, many names for this technique, but they are basically all the same.) These students were shown how to *see* themselves scoring well on their tests and thoroughly enjoying the
experience of learning. The second group was taught in the usual
way. The results—to the surprise of the skeptical but to the delight
of all—were higher scores and a greater excitement about learning
than ever before by the group taught mental imaging.

Your mind is like a tape recorder, carefully taking down everything you say and think and acting on those beliefs. If what you seek
is good health, *picture* your body glowing and radiant. *See* yourself in
a new house; *say* to yourself, "I am becoming slimmer and trimmer";
know that you will conquer your fear of flying. It will all be taken in
by your mind, and your beliefs will become your destiny.

The more you develop this imaging skill, the faster the universe will respond, by making your dreams come true. Remember
that your conscious mind is finite (limited), while the God-force is
infinite (unlimited). Therefore, Creative Intelligence intercedes
whenever necessary to boost your creative imaging energy into achieving even better results. If you want to marry John Doe but that
doesn't happen, have faith that God has someone better for you.
Sometimes, the longer it takes your mental images to produce results, the bigger they are.

Always be aware that imaging can work miraculously or disastrously for you, depending on what you image on a regular basis. (Do you image lack and failure or abundance and success?) Whatever is happening in your life now is a reflection of some previous image that evolved from your mind. *Even if your conscious, reasoning mind feels you are not worthy to receive these positive images or that it is not possible for you to attain your goal, your mental pictures—if imagined enough—will overpower your conscious reasoning.*

Be cautious of what you imagine for others, as well, and make sure you picture what *you* want, rather than what someone else wants or thinks you need to experience.

21. *The Law of Order.* Throughout the universe, there is divine order. A chaotic, cluttered environment produces chaotic, cluttered reactions in our minds. You cannot utilize your full potential in such a state. We must, therefore, be careful to be orderly, organized, and disciplined in our daily routines. This applies to our relationships and our children, as well as our homes, cars, and offices. You must prove to the Higher Intelligence that you are worthy to receive better things, so you must keep in order what you already have. Once again, old folk sayings are seen for their kernels of truth: Remember your grandmother telling you "Cleanliness is next to Godliness"?

One of the great achievements of civilization is the alphabetic system by which we are able to file and *order* a large number of elements. The Law of Order emphasizes the importance of this ability, as we consider and organize our goals. (Imagine what it would be like to try to keep track of things without an alphabetic or numeric system!)

22. *The Law of Persistence.* Persistence and patience go hand in hand. You must persist in the drive for attainment of your goals while patiently waiting for results. Persistence is the determined effort to bring about fulfillment. The Law of Persistence enables those who chase dreams to catch them.

Many times, if you persist just a little longer, you can get what you want. When you don't follow through, you can lose out on a lot of opportunities. Lao-tzu, the Chinese writer of the sixth century B.C., said, "People usually fail when they are on the verge of success, so give as much care to the end as to the beginning." When highly successful people are interviewed, they invariably say that without persistence they would have gotten nowhere. Often, this means a great deal of hard work, but the persistence always pays off—sometimes in unexpected ways.

The book *Zen and the Art of Motorcycle Maintenance*, a cult classic of the 1960s that ultimately sold over six million copies, was rejected by 150 publishers before it was taken; Sally Jessy Raphaël, now one of the country's top-rated television talk show hostesses, was fired from fifteen radio jobs before she landed her television contract. In both cases, persistence paid off. It is only when we *expect* things to come easily that we are disappointed and often fail. Knowing in advance that the Law of Persistence is immutable will help you to keep a steady handle on your progress and to not expect too much too soon.

23. *The Law of Praise.* Praising is the quickest way to turn around the negative aspects of your life. You should praise the God-force for *all* things, whether you consider them positive or negative, good or bad. (This theory actually goes back to the ancient Talmud of the Jews.) People usually talk to God only in times of need. They forget to thank Him for all things. But if you don't praise Him for all things, the flow of your prosperity may become blocked. No matter what you are experiencing—emotional or financial problems, happiness or tragedy—give thanks to God, knowing that whatever happens in your life is serving to educate you and bring you closer to your final destination: becoming one with the Creative Intelligence.

After my clairaudient (hearing) unfoldment in 1971, God continued to speak to me in response to my requests for help with unhappy situations. When I would say, "Please help me with this," or "Please help me with that," He would say, "Don't ask me for help first. Praise me first, for the problem." He told me this several times, and although I heard and understood this universal principle, it was hard for me to practice it at all times. I would still find myself grumbling about certain things without praising God. It was just so difficult for me to praise Him for some of those negative things. Then, in 1975, while I was teaching physical education, I was assigned the school library as an office, due to lack of space. One day, while programming my mind for good things to manifest, I walked by the librarian's desk, where a small yellow book attracted my attention. The title was *The Power of Praise*, by Merlin Carothers, an Army chaplain. I picked it up and opened it intuitively to the message I was supposed to receive. (This often happens to me, with books, as I allow God to reveal messages to me in this manner.)

The first paragraph I saw read, "*Praise*, according to Webster's dictionary, means to extol, laud, honor, acclaim, or express approval of something. Giving our approval means that we accept or agree with what we approve of. So to praise God for a difficult situation, a sickness or disaster, means literally that we accept and approve of its happening, as part of God's plan for our lives."

We cannot really praise God without being thankful for the things for which we are praising Him. And we cannot really be thankful without being happy about what we're thankful for. Praising, then, involves both gratitude and joy. It is not always easy to praise God, especially when we're going through tough times, but it is important to know that praising God speeds up the process of achieving what you desire. Just remember that, while you may not be particularly happy about a specific event in your life, the joy comes from knowing that God is helping you to ultimately reach your goals.

The very fact that we praise God, and not some unknown fate, also means that we accept that God is responsible for what is happening. Otherwise, it would make little sense to thank Him for it. Any form of sincere prayer opens the door for God's power to move into our lives. But the power of prayer releases more of God's power than any other form of petition. The Bible gives examples which demonstrate this fact again and again: "But Thou art holy, O Thou that inhabitest the praises of Israel." (Psalms 22:3) No wonder God's power and presence is near when we praise Him. He actually dwells, inhabits, resides in our praises!

After reading *The Power of Praise*, I picked up another of Carothers's books, *Prison to Praise*, in which he says, "I have come to believe that the prayer of praise is the highest form of communication with God, and one that always releases a great deal of power into our lives. Praising Him is not something we do because we feel good; rather, it is an act of obedience. Often the prayer of praise is done out of sheer teeth-gritting willpower; yet, when we persist in it, somehow the power of God is released into us and into the situation, first in a trickle, perhaps, but later in growing streams that finally flood us and wash away the old hurts and scars."

After reading that passage, I realized how lackadaisical I had been in my praise of God, and I began to fervently apply these principles to my everyday life.

For many years I suffered from migraine headaches. When I learned to praise God for all things, even in the midst of crying and vomiting I would mentally and audibly praise Him by saying, "Thank you, God, for the headache I am having right now. I know there is a reason for this and that something good will come of it. I know that you are guiding me toward the right situations and the right solutions. Whatever is necessary to eliminate my headaches, I know it will be manifest more quickly as a result of my praising. I am not lazy. I will work hard and put forth the effort in what I am guided to do. I am asking for an immediate healing of this headache."

I praised God for all circumstances, and things began to work out faster and better than before. One day, while I was standing in line at a health-food store, two people next to me were discussing their success with just such a problem, helped by a specialist in deep neuromuscular treatment. I asked for his name, went to see him, and got what seemed miraculous relief. That same week, at a bookstore, a book on migraines and how to help yourself out of them literally fell into my hands off the shelf! Truly, God works in wondrous ways.

A client came to me because of a problem with her job. She mentioned that she'd been in an accident, that her car had been damaged, and that she could no longer drive it. She was angry at the man who hit her and at her insurance company. The last thing on her mind was praising God. I told this client that praising God was the first thing she should have done, and together we thanked Him for the difficulties she was having. When she left, I suggested a couple of good garages where she could have her car repaired. About a month later, she called me again. She said that stopping at the garage was the best thing that ever happened to her. A man at the shop, also getting his car fixed, was the head of a large company and was looking for a new account executive. He gave her the job, she loved it, and she was making double her old salary.

That client's story is but one example of how the Law of Praise works. Many people have turned situations far worse than hers into positive circumstances. (See the Law of Transmutation.) Again and again, you hear of people who have been injured or disabled and then go on to achieve so much through activities that often are a result of their dramatic situation.

It is extremely difficult for me (I'm human, too!) to praise God for all situations. But I know how very important this Law is, so I do my best to follow it, even as I am constantly working on being sincere about my praising. Sometimes, I fall short, but I have found that, if you start with smaller circumstances, it soon becomes a habit. Sincere praising is the highest indication of faith.

To my knowledge, no studies have been done comparing those who praise with those who don't, but I feel certain that those who do will experience greater improvement, faster, in their lives. As you praise, the Creative Force enlightens your mind, revealing what is to be learned from these experiences. This, in turn, increases your self-awareness and confidence. The positive outcome evolves more quickly, and the enlightenment opens the way to healing.

The Law of Praise is one of the most difficult to master, but as praising God becomes a habit, you will overcome all the negative aspects of your life. To remind myself of the importance of praising, I have compiled my own praise list, which I keep with me and frequently update. Your list might look like this:

FRUSTRATIONS, VOIDS, LACKS, AND NEGATIVE CIRCUMSTANCES	OPPORTUNITIES, BLESSINGS, AND POSITIVE CIRCUMSTANCES
Thank you: • That I've just had an argument with my boss. • That I haven't received the check I'm waiting for yet. • That I haven't been able to lose weight. • That I don't have a romantic companion in my life now. • That my car was stolen.	Thank you: • That I have a good job near my home. • That my mother is recovering well from her operation. • That I seem to be in good health. • That I had a wonderful vacation in Hawaii. • That many profitable opportunities have opened up for me.

- That I have a lot of bills and I'm afraid I won't have enough money to pay them.
- That I lack self-confidence.

- That I have friends who are caring, considerate, and honest.
- That my loan went through at the bank.

24. *The Law of Prayer.* Prayer *does* change things. It is the form of spiritual communication in which you speak directly to the Creator (as opposed to meditation, which is "listening"). The divine power of prayer cannot be overemphasized. Prayer is the catalyst that accelerates all the constructive forces necessary to bring about speedy results, subject to divine order. To keep an open and clear line of communication, we must eradicate impurities of mind, body, and spirit.

Emmet Fox, author and religious educator, describes how the wondrous power of prayer works for whatever you want: "Prayer does change things. Prayer does make things happen quite otherwise than they would have happened had the prayer not been made. It makes no difference at all what sort of difficulty you may be in. It does not matter what the causes may have been that led up to it. Enough prayer will get you out of difficulty, if only you will be persistent enough in your appeal of God."

Julian Whitaker, M.D., reports in a commentary titled *Does Prayer Help Healing?*, that "Larry Dossey, M.D., author of *Healing Words,* writes how astonished he was to find over 100 published studies—using good science—of which over half showed that prayer brings about significant changes in a variety of living beings. The book documents the far-reaching power of prayer." He goes on to say: "Dr. Dossey reports that any form of prayer, regardless of [religious] faith, is beneficial." Whitaker also mentions that one of the most significant studies on prayer was carried out by Randolph Byrd,

M.D., in 1988. In a carefully controlled experiment, 393 people admitted to the coronary care unit at San Francisco General Hospital were randomly divided into two groups. One group received intercessory prayer from church groups; the other group was the control. After extensive evaluation, it was found that those who received prayer "fared significantly better. There are only two explanations for the improved status of the prayer group," he says: "(1) it occurred due to chance, or (2) it occurred as the result of prayer. The odds of its being due to chance, however, were one in 10,000. Therefore, unless you believe that this study just happened to hit that one in 10,000, me difference can be attributed to prayer. Had this been the evaluation of a new drug designed to improve the overall status of patients in coronary care units, it would be heralded as a breakthrough and rushed into service." Whitaker's full and further discussion may be found in the April 1994 edition of his newsletter, *Health & Healing*.

The Byrd study shows the power of prayer for others as well as for ourselves.

I also pray for those who have passed on, because they are helped and uplifted by prayer power. Prayer affects their vibratory level, as it does ours, and assists them in their evolutionary process on the other side. I also believe that many prayers and positive thoughts are sent to us from this other dimension, and that it is, therefore, important that we remain open and receptive to receiving those energies.

When it seems that a prayer is not answered, the energy spent is not wasted. Instead, it is recycled (transmuted) into bigger and better things for you.

25. *The Law of Productivity.* Man develops and grows through productivity. We should perform our work in life as well as we can, even if we encounter great difficulties in the process. God rewards those who persevere and work hard. It gives you a great feeling of

satisfaction when you do things well and have been productive. Whatever you do, strive for high productivity and high quality in all areas.

In the book *Children of Paradise: Successful Parenting for Prosperous Families,* author Lee Hausner explains the necessity of real and productive projects, even for children growing up in wealthy and comfortable circumstances. Just as the "idle rich" often turned to alcohol and drugs, and just as Gloria Vanderbilt described herself as "a poor little rich girl" before she went into business, so will we all lose our way without work we deem important and useful. This has nothing to do with the amount of money one is paid but, rather, with the real life value of the endeavor. Hence, the woman or man who chooses to stay home and raise children is just as productive as one earning a large salary in the business world. We may well wonder whatever happened to the theory that "anything worth doing is worth doing well," considering the shoddy workmanship and lack of concern we encounter in today's workplace, but every poll ever taken among workers in the United States has shown that the greatest job satisfaction exists where productivity is the highest.

26. *The Law of Release.* Detaching yourself from a disagreeable circumstance allows change and improvement in your life. The situation needs to be released to God so higher power can help work through the problem and heal it. Lack of release will keep you chained to the circumstance, which causes interference with your progress. Fear, and lack of faith, keep us from releasing. The universe is waiting for us to release *in faith.* Only then can we receive.

Using the Law of Emotional Detachment, we free ourselves from thoughts about people. We then can redirect our energies and focus on other things.

How many times have you heard it said that someone seems "addicted" to another person in an unhealthy and unproductive (for the addicted person) relationship? Through the Law of Release, and with faith in God, that harmful bond can be severed and the former addict directed to a healthy, productive, and fulfilling relationship.

Surrounding yourself with positive people is very important in helping you disengage from an emotionally charged situation, while God works on healing it. Surround yourself with white light, for spiritual energy, while visualizing yourself detached from the person and situation. Praise God for the problem, and remember to call upon other people to assist you through prayer.

An otherwise bright and very well-educated woman once came to see me about her desperately unhappy marriage. She was angry, frustrated, and physically ill from the stress of the relationship and the outrageous behavior of her husband. But, she said, she "has trouble with separation" and so put up with a truly untenable situation. It wasn't even a question of money, as is so often the case. She simply couldn't let go. After months of discussion and prayer and resuscitating the religious faith she once had had, she finally was able to "Let Go and Let God." It was scary, for her, but she is now a new person—with a new look and confidence about her and a whole new, holistic life ahead of her.

27. *The Law of Substitution.* This law is closely related to the Vacuum Law of Prosperity and the Law of Release, as once a situation is released, a void is created through the Vacuum Law of Prosperity. At this point the Law of Substitution takes effect. It is the general nature of the universe to fill any voids ("Nature abhors a vacuum"), in order to maintain harmony and balance. If you dare to think big and visualize your dreams, you may receive them in place of what you just released. This substitution can be even better if you program for it. It is also the basis for the saying, "God never closes one door in your life without opening another one."

I know a woman who was depressed because the new lawn

mower for which she had worked so hard was stolen. When her friends invited her to a function at a local club she didn't feel like going, but she remembered what I had told her, previously, about forcing herself to go out and start changing her attitude. She thanked God for the problem and went out with her friends. It turned out the club was having a drawing for door prizes, and she was one of the winners. Out of all the prizes, hers was a year's free lawn service! Coincidence? No. That is what the Law of Substitution can do for you.

28. *The Law of Thrift and Conservation.* To be of maximum use to others as well as to ourselves, we should economize on time, energy, and money. This particular law goes hand in hand with the Law of Productivity for, as you conserve your time, energy, and money, you will become more productive. A daily plan detailing what you want (and intend!) to accomplish is important for your time/energy management. A budget is helpful for your financial management. Waste and frivolous spending are contrary to universal law; they karmically block the flow of prosperity.

Ellen, a college student out on her own for the first time in her life, had a very wise father. Knowing his daughter to be a basically reliable and straight-thinking young woman, he wanted to increase her sense of responsibility and teach her the value of budgeting her funds wisely. Rather than pay her bills or give her a certain amount of spending money each month, he had her open a bank account in her own name alone, and gave her a sum of money he thought would last her the year. Then he told her, "This money is yours. Use what you need and, if it is short, let me know. But if it is sufficient, whatever you have left over at the end of the year is yours to keep." Needless to say, Ellen used her funds both carefully and wisely and did, in fact, have some remaining at the end of the school term. So wise had *she* become, by this time, she left the funds to collect interest and had even more to use for a special trip at the end of her second year.

29. *The Law of Transmutation.* The word *transmutation* means "to change over." This applies holistically to your mind, body, and spirit. In other words, you can change negative energies into positive ones. Allow every negative experience in your life to become positive and you will find that even through unhappy experiences you will discover happiness. I often refer to this as *divine discontent.*

Examples of the validity of this Law appear almost weekly in papers like *The Wall Street Journal,* whose pages are full of stories of middle and top executives who were fired from their lucrative jobs and forced to find other work. Time and time again we read comments such as, "I thought it was the end of the world, but it was the best thing that ever happened to me." This is just the story I heard from Robert, formerly associated with a Fortune 500 company. "I decided to pursue an idea and a dream I've had for many years, and I started my own business," he told me. "Not knowing whether I'd be able to afford rent, I set up an office in my home, where I now see more of my wife and children and actually participate in their lives. My little business is growing nicely. I'm my own boss, as well as the bookkeeper and expediter. I'm not making the money I was before, but I've never been happier in my life!" This is a man who has discovered what the Law of Transmutation can do.

A close friend of mine had a renter staying at her house for a short time and was upset when he told her he had to leave. Since she needed the extra income he was providing, she and I both meditated intensely that the situation be transmuted into something positive for her. Within three days she had a call from her aunt, who knew someone who wanted to move in. Within a very short time, this landlord/tenant relationship turned into a friendship, so not only did my friend have the income, she had a great new friend.

One terribly tragic circumstance that was transmuted into something good was the abduction of six-year-old Adam Walsh from a Florida mall several years ago. His parents discovered how inadequate the system was in locating missing children. There was no coordination on any level of government. After the gruesome discovery of Adam's body, the Walshes determined to improve the system. They formed the Adam Walsh Child Resource Center and have truly opened the nation's eyes to the problem of missing children. Although it was too late for little Adam, their tragedy has no doubt saved the lives of many other youngsters. The Walshes transmuted their intense pain in such a way that the whole world was affected.

30. *The Vacuum Law of Prosperity.* Also known as the Law of Release, this law—coined by Catherine Ponder in her book *The Dynamic Laws of Prosperity*—allows us to fill our individual needs to their fullest capacity. Ponder tells us, "Get rid of what you don't want and make room for what you do want. Create a space, a vacuum, and believe and expect it will be filled, and it will be." This includes getting rid of both unnecessary material and negative emotional baggage. If you need new furnishings, according to this law, first get rid of the old, and the Vacuum Law of Prosperity will take over. In the same way, if you release unconstructive ideas, prosperity will be yours.

I used to be a pack rat, keeping and saving everything I could get my hands on, even if I didn't need it. Now I have learned that the more I give freely and openly, the more I receive. Now I clean and clear my closets, drawers, and cupboards of everything I don't need or use, and I give the things away to people who can use them. Not only does that make me feel good, it also opens the door for new things to come to me. The same is true for relationships. If it's not good, release it. Either it will work out or something better will come your way.

It is difficult to release someone or something before something or someone else comes into your life. It takes a tremendous amount of faith, but I have seen over and over again the positive effect it has had on my life and the life of those around me.

Remember that *faith is synergistic: The more you believe, the more will come to you. And the more that comes to you, the more you will believe.*

A client named Shirley was in a relationship that was far from ideal. In fact, Shirley was miserable. But she didn't want to let go of even this poor companion until she'd met someone else and, thus far, there was no one else who interested her. She had a lot going for her, but her anxiety at spending some weekends alone overrode her good sense. After a good deal of counseling, she realized that letting go of her disquieting relationship would have to be her first step in achieving a wholistic life. Once she did, she felt much better and, two months later—when her life was in order again—she met someone new.

Prosperous Thinking gives you the power to make your dreams come true. It extends the concept of mental imaging so that your thoughts radiate into the universe. As you clear your mind of negative thoughts, to let the positive images in, so—as you rid your physical environment of unnecessary clutter—you will make room for all the bounty your heart and mind desire.

31. *The Law of Vision.* Vision is intelligent foresight. It is the ability to look at something and see the possibilities. Always have a goal; then envision yourself as an integral part in the universal plan. From research, facts, experiences, and meditation, you will be able to make wise choices to further your ultimate goals. Your belief in yourself and in your vision will help to create what you want to be.

The best interior designers and real estate investors are the ones with the vision to look at a dilapidated house or building and vividly imagine what can be done to improve it. If you look at most successful entrepreneurs, they're the ones with the vision, persistence, and intelligence to turn an idea into a profit-making venture.

Usually, acting on vision entails a certain amount of risk. To turn vision into reality, it is necessary to spend time, energy, and or money without a guarantee that your idea will pan out. For this reason, using your intuitive ability will help you to determine whether your vision will be a success. After that, reduce your risk with the determined application of the universal laws.

In the area of Miami Beach now known worldwide as "South Beach" or the "Art Deco District," the buildings so popular in the 1930s and 1940s had fallen into disrepair and the neighborhood was derelict. Today, as a result of the vision of the late Barbara Capitman and the determination of a core group of citizens, developers, and restaurateurs, South Beach is one of the hottest real estate markets in the world and a mecca for filmmakers, models, and gourmets. It was the people with *vision* who were able to take advantage of the area's lush possibilities.

Part Three

SPIRITUAL
AND PSYCHIC
DEVELOPMENT

Blessed are they that have not seen, and yet have believed.
—JESUS CHRIST

Human beings can alter their lives by altering their
attitudes of mind.
—WILLIAM JAMES

Everybody reaps the fruit of his own deeds.
—BHAGAVATA PURANA 10.4.18

There is only one religion, though there are a hundred
versions of it.

—GEORGE BERNARD SHAW

All things are filled full of signs, and it is a wise man who
can learn about one thing from another.

—PLOTINUS

If any man among you seem to be religious, and bridleth
not his tongue, but deceiveth his own heart, this man's
religion is vain.

—JAMES 1:26

Chapter One

SPIRITUALITY AND FAITH

RELIGION

Throughout the ages, man has sought to understand himself and his purpose on earth. He endlessly examines his relationship with a Higher Intelligence with whom he has somehow learned to communicate. He interprets these communications in many ways. This desire to understand God and the universe is the basis for all religions.

In the holistic philosophy of religion, spiritual well-being is emphasized as a necessary part of the whole. To be truly holistic, you must be in tune with the Creator. Everyone's purpose in life is to become closer to this Higher Intelligence.

There is so much to learn about spirituality that we can never know all the answers in our lifetime. This is why my own beliefs are not limited to one religious doctrine. My beliefs grow and change according to my spiritual awakening. My purpose in discussing this topic is not to attempt to convert anyone to my beliefs but, rather, to awaken in each reader a curiosity and a willingness to learn about spirituality and the part it plays in each of our lives. There are many valid organized religions in the world, and I believe each has a purpose and a place.

Religions evolved in the same way people have evolved through the ages: Church doctrines and texts have changed dramatically, during centuries of revision. In addition, Eastern religions have been brought to the West and have begun to gain acceptance. Terms such as *reincarnation* and *karma* are now understood almost universally. The fact that religions may disagree in certain aspects doesn't mean one is right and the other wrong. Different religions should be looked upon as different paths to the same goal: spiritual perfection.

Many religions believe in God and Jesus, but minor theological differences have led to major conflicts among them. There is no need for religions to clash. Wars based on religious differences are an affront to God. We are all God's children; He loves us all equally and wants harmony in his universe. Each religion has its own version of "The Golden Rule." If we would all live by it faithfully, we would never have the bloody wars we have today and have had throughout history. Religion should provide comfort and direction for its adherents, rather than competition, power plays, and territorial disputes.

According to *The World Almanac*, there are (in round numbers) some 760 million people in the world who consider themselves Christians (all denominations). There are close to one billion followers of Islam (Muslims); 700 million Hindus; 300 million Buddhists; 5 million Confucianists; 3 million Shintoists; and 17 million Jews. Each religion is in some way based on becoming closer to the Higher Intelligence.

A large number of people in the world don't belong to any organized religion, yet see themselves as very spiritual. A recent Gallup poll revealed that "86% of the 'unchurched' and 76% of churchgoers agreed that individuals should arrive at their beliefs outside organized religions." The poll also found that about 60 percent of churchgoers agreed with the statement, "Most churches have lost the real spiritual part of religion." This reflects poorly on the state of organized churches and religions, some of which seem to devote more time to temporal and political issues than to the spiritual development of their members.

It is interesting to note that one of the oldest pieces of metaphysical material in existence finds its origin in Judaism. The *Kabbalah,* comprising nearly three thousand books that its authors attribute to inspiration and messengers from the other dimension, deals with many subjects considered a part of modern metaphysics and parapsychology: Reincarnation, meditation, astral projection, healing, astrology, magic, karma, and psychic energy are examples. (It should be noted that only the ultra-orthodox Hasidim, among Jews today, actively follow Kabbalistic principles, although more and more Jews are undertaking the study of this fascinating text. The Kabbalah Learning Centre—founded in Jerusalem in 1922—describes the books of the Kabbalah as "giving us knowledge about the ways to unleash and maximize all our hidden potential and create a more spiritual, balanced and rewarding life for ourselves and our families.")

In sum, there are many spiritual paths, all of which lead to the same destination. Each of us must find me one which feels right to us. The important thing is to *find* one and *follow* it.

PSYCHIC PHENOMENA IN THE BIBLE

Every form of psychic phenomenon may be found in the Bible, as every religion is based on extrasensory experiences. Without these psychic phenomena there would be no religions: The mind would be unable to communicate with any Higher Intelligence. In all religions, this communication is achieved by prayer and meditation— practices accepted by any spiritual person. In the absence of such communication there would be no prophecy, revelation, miracle healings, clairvoyance, or clairaudience. The medieval Jewish philosopher Maimonides (1135–1204) was the first known scholar to explain the basis of prophecy as a natural human ability. Pope Benedict XIV (1675–1758; elected 1730), known as the Father of Christian Parapsychology, expressed similar beliefs. Influenced by this pope, a German priest named Johannes Greber published *Communication with the Spirit World* in 1930.

In his article "Vision and Audition in Biblical Prophecy," written in 1978, Boyce M. Bennett, Jr., professor of the Old Testament at the General Theological Seminary, in New York, wrote: "When we begin to examine the Bible in terms of the categories of the paranormal, we are confronted with an almost embarrassing abundance of parapsychological riches. Examples of telepathy, clairvoyance, precognition, mediumship, psychokinesis, and out-of-body experiences abound. . . . There has never been any question that the ancient world believed in the paranormal, even though they would not have used such a descriptive term."

In other words, the ancients did not consider these phenomena anything but *normal!* It is worth asking why and when we lost our willingness to accept these experiences as common to man. When did these occurrences—so easily accepted in ancient times—become strange and unnatural to us?

Following are some examples taken from the Bible:

CLAIRAUDIENCE: "When Paul was told by a supernormal voice to remain in the city of Corinth preaching, he stayed" (Acts 18:9).

TRANCE OR DREAMLIKE STATE: "When Paul was entranced and directed to leave the town of Jerusalem for they would not receive his testimony, he left" (Acts 22:18).

CLAIRVOYANCE: "When Paul was called to Macedonia through a supernormal vision he went at once to the city" (Acts 16:9).

PROPHECY OR PRECOGNITION: "Peter said unto Him, 'Lord why cannot I follow Thee now? I will lay down my life for Thy sake.' Jesus answered him, 'Wilt thou lay down thy life for my sake? Verily, verily, I say unto thee, the cock shall not crow, till thou has denied me thrice'" (John 13:37–38).

TELEPATHY: "Then there arose a reasoning among them, which of them should be the greatest. And Jesus, perceiving the thought of their hearts. . . ." (Luke 9:46–47).

CLAIRVOYANCE: "And Jesus, when he was Baptized, went up straightaway out of the water: and, lo, the heavens were opened unto Him, and He saw the Spirit of God descending like a dove, and lightning upon Him" (Matthew 3:16).

CLAIRAUDIENCE: "And lo a voice from heaven, saying, 'This is my beloved Son, in whom I am well pleased'" (Matthew 3:17).

SPIRIT MATERIALIZATION: "And after eight days again His disciples within, and Thomas with them, then came Jesus, the doors being shut. . . . Then said He unto Thomas, 'Reach hither thy finger and behold my hands; and reach hither thy hand and thrust it into my side'" (John 20:26–27, after Jesus' physical death).

"And in the fourth watch of the night Jesus went up to them, walking on the seas. . . . And when the disciples saw Him walking on the sea, they were troubled, saying, 'It is a spirit'" (Matthew 14:25–26).

"And (He) was transfigured before them: and His face did shine as the sun, and His raiment was white as the light" (Matthew 17:1–2).

Clairvoyant visions and "speaking in tongues" are abundant in the Bible, as they are in our world today (although many people, today, mistakenly fear both to be some form of Satanism). All the prophets in the Bible had such experiences, which were truly God-inspired. Moses had numerous such experiences:

> "And it came to pass, when Moses came down from Mount Sinai . . . that Moses wist not that the skin of his face shown while he talked with him" (Aaron) (Exodus 34:29).
> "And the Lord came down in a cloud and spake unto him, and took of the spirit that was upon him, and gave it unto the seventy elders" (Numbers 11:25).
> "And the angel of the Lord appeared unto him in a flame of fire out of the midst of a bush" (Exodus 3 :2).

The materialization of spirits and angels occurs throughout the Bible. An angel materialized at the tomb of Jesus; Jesus materialized to the disciples and for Mary Magdalene; when Peter was in prison, an angel materialized and actually struck him; and, of course, in one of the most impressive of acts, Jesus materialized fishes and loaves of bread for the multitude.

ANGELS

According to a recent poll, some 80 percent of Americans believe they have "guardian angels" who protect them. Angels were created by God to assist Him with His universe. Found in almost all the world's religions, they work to bring and maintain peace, harmony, and love. Used properly (we must learn to *ask* for their assistance), they help to remove the burdens we bear and achieve the goals we seek.

Each of us has at least two angels assigned to us. Some—usually those with a special mission—have more. They are always at your side, though you may be completely unaware of them, and their purpose is to protect you and to help you progress as rapidly as possible to a higher plane of existence. We must ask and then be open to their help, knowing that that help may come in a variety of ways. Those who are open are assisted in their daily lives without being conscious of it. The most common means of communicating with us is through impressions or "fleeting thoughts." For example, you may be planning to take a certain route or run a certain errand, when the thought comes to you to do something else, first. That change in plans may, in fact, save you *from* something or lead you *to* something, to your benefit.

It's true there is no way of proving any of this, and many see it as pure coincidence. But a person would have to be extremely lucky to avoid all the hazardous circumstances of life without divine guidance. And how often someone says, at times like these, "I must have a guardian angel" or "Someone up there was watching over me."

It is up to you to get in touch with your own personal angels and allow them to help. There are several things you can do to communicate with them:

1. Have a deep desire to establish communication.
2. Meditate.
3. Keep an angel journal. Write down your goals and desires and assign angels to more specific areas. As you get results, make notations. You will soon notice the angels at work.
4. Have faith and use visualization techniques. Imagine meeting an angel; imagine what the angel will look, smell, and feel like; imagine what you will discuss with the angel; visualize floating into the

etheric realm and flying with the angels through all the heavenly colors; record all your experiences, impressions, thoughts, and feelings.

5. Relax and pay attention to the angels helping you.
6. Call upon your angels to keep you on course and to remove doubt and fear.
7. Write to your angels. Tell them what you want from them, what it is you want them to understand, how you want them to react and what you want them to do. After you write your letter, put it in a special place: in a Bible, a special book, a jewelry box, etc.

The next step is to become open to communication *from* your guardian angels. It does no good for them to offer help if you ignore their assistance. Think of how many times a thought has crossed your mind that you ignored, only to find that what you *thought* actually transpired. Recently, I had to take my car to be fixed and thought I might have to wait awhile before someone picked me up. The thought crossed my mind to be sure to take a book with me, but I didn't act on it. I didn't go right over to the book I wanted to read and put it with my purse and keys. The result was that I forgot to take the book and was stuck waiting for over an hour with nothing to do.

There is a story about a man living along a flooding river. He was told to evacuate but said he wasn't worried, that God would take care of him. As the river rose, a rescue team came for him, but again he refused, saying God would protect him. The river began to crest, and once more a rescue team came, pleading with him to leave. But as before, this man of faith declined. When the river covered his roof, he drowned. Having led a good life, he went to heaven, where he asked God how He could have abandoned him, in his hour of need. God told him, "What do you mean, abandoned? Three times I sent you salvation."

It is not enough to ask; we must listen and watch for the answers. Responses come in many forms: intuition; opportunities; sometimes feelings, such as confidence and peace of mind.

Once you are in the habit of communicating with your angels, you will find yourself in constant conversation with them. Never doubt that they are there for you. And remember, always, to praise and thank them for their guidance.

SPIRIT GUIDES

Spirit guides are on a level somewhat below that of angelic representatives and therefore have different powers, but in all cases they work in conjunction to benefit the individual and humanity. Some spirit guides are friends, family, or loved ones who have passed on and who come in and out of our lives periodically to assist us. On the other side—where they have their own angels, guides, and teachers—they themselves work to evolve, learn, and grow. As beings who have lived here before and who have experienced some of our problems, they assist themselves by using their energies to help us. As you ask their assistance and make use of their ability to help, you will find they render your life more ordered and less haphazard. They are the voice of experience through which we can make our own lives that much less stressful.

I was once driving along a rather wide road, on my way to vote. Although I was undoubtedly thinking about the day's election, I was paying my usual attention to driving, especially as this was a neighborhood new to me. Approaching a cross street narrower than the one I was on, I suddenly realized that a car coming across, from my left, did not appear to be slowing down to stop. Under normal circumstances I would have slammed on my brakes to avoid a collision, but "something" (someone?) told me to *jam down my accelerator and get out of his way.* Had I *braked,* we surely would have collided in the center, and one or both of us might have been killed. I had never before thought to accelerate at such a time, and—looking back—I have to believe it was a spirit guide, who—having been here before—knew just what I should do and sent the message to do it.

Why else should you develop a relationship with God, angels and spiritual guides? You will be happier and have a more fulfilled life, and you will reach your goals faster. Whatever you seek will be experienced more harmoniously. This doesn't mean you will be free of problems and difficulties, but, by allowing them into your life and feeling their energy pass through you, you will overcome those problems and difficulties with a confidence and success impossible otherwise.

It is important to relax and *know* this guidance is available to you, rather than become preoccupied with whether or not you are "getting through." As the Bible says, "Seek and ye shall find." You have but to ask, with sincerity and good intention, and then to remain open for the answers to come to you.

CULTS

As you seek like-minded, well-intentioned individuals with whom you can share your experiences, beware that you are not drawn into one of the many cults that have, unfortunately, infected our society.

A cult is a system of religious ritual or obsessive devotion to a person or principle. Not all cults are negative. Religious cults have always existed, and many of today's religions were first considered cults. But while there are those that help society's outcasts and give them shelter in a positive way, there are more that take even previously well-adjusted people and render them virtually unable to function in society.

Cults are dangerous when they deny people the right to exercise free will. Through brainwashing and programming techniques, they thrive on mandatory "donations" from their members, who become fanatical in their devotion to the leader and the cult community. Many of these leaders claim to be psychic or spiritual, but rather than encourage their followers to develop their own abilities, they use their usually impressive leadership abilities to manipulate the behavior of their adherents. In a number of cults, members' names are changed to something unusual but reverent-sounding (usually of an Eastern-religious nature).

In today's society, it is sometimes difficult to distinguish a legitimate religion from a cult. Cult members no longer necessarily wear robes, shave their heads, or look any different from most people. Who could have imagined that nine hundred "normal" people would commit mass suicide in Jonestown, Guyana?

Recruiting techniques can be very subtle, but they are always manipulative. They generally tend to appeal to the downtrodden—those without direction, who cannot adjust to society's norms, and who give themselves over, mentally and financially, to a stronger person who offers easy redemption. Cults usually require total, slavelike devotion to the group or the group leader. The initiation process is very intense; members must learn unconditional obedience to the cult's rules and purpose. When a large group of people unite their energies in such a way, the collective potential to do good or harm is enormous. Unfortunately, in most cases, what's done is harm. Children leave and turn on their parents; parents abandon their families; siblings attack one another. No room is allowed for dissent; no argument against the cult—however reasoned—is tolerated.

True religious leaders can be easily differentiated from cult leaders, as all true religions are based on the doing of God's will, and true leaders will encourage us to love one another and be true to ourselves. This means we have the free will to make our own decisions and also that we will be held responsible for our actions.

LIFE AFTER DEATH

What happens after we die is one of life's eternal mysteries. No one really knows for sure until he himself dies, but some interesting theories and experiences abound. I believe there is an existence beyond our own life. In recent years, through well-researched accounts of "near-death experiences," more information has become available regarding what this life after death might be like. Although different people have different experiences, there are sufficient similarities among them that scientists no longer can ignore their probable validity.

A 1981 Gallup poll revealed that two-thirds of adult Americans (approximately 100 million people) believe that life exists beyond death. Some 23 million claim to have had a "verge of death" or "temporary death" experience (so named because, just before the final passing over, they returned to life). Of those 23 million, 8 million experienced some kind of mystical encounter at the time of near-death.

The majority of people who describe near-death cite one or more of the following details:

- a calm, peaceful feeling.
- an out-of-body sensation, in which they hovered above their own body and sometimes observed efforts to revive them.
- a feeling of traveling down a long, dark tunnel with a dazzling, brilliant white light at the end.
- entering the light to find a world of unforgettable and extraordinary beauty, often with lovely gardens and landscapes, ethereal music, and reunions with deceased relatives or friends.
- the presence of an all-loving being or energy.

- the presence of loved ones who already have passed on.
- awareness of activities going on outside the body while in an unconscious state.
- premonitions of future events.
- a sense of painlessness.
- the impression of reviewing or reexamining one's life in vivid detail, in a brief, highly compressed period of time.
- a special sensation of being in another world.

When Dr. Raymond Moody, Jr., published accounts of some fifty near-death experiences in his book, *Life After Life*, interest in this subject soared and more and more people, in all walks of life, reported similar occurrences. Although the reports in Moody's book are "anecdotal" rather than scientific, he claims all the experiences are authentic.

Since the publication of Moody's book, scientists have used their own approach to prove or refute his claims, with some fascinating results. In one instance, Dr. Michael Sabom, of Atlanta, set out to *disprove* Moody's findings and, instead, ended by writing his own book, *Reflections on Death*, which *echoed* many of the results Moody found. Sabom does differ with Moody in that he believes the experience of *death* is not necessarily the same as that of *near-death*, that there may be a separation of the mind from the physical brain at death.

It has been reported that close to 35 percent of those who come close to death have an NDE—Near Death Experience. They normally occur under such circumstances as:

- being close to death
- physical accidents, injuries, and illness
- childbirth

- hospital operations
- criminal attacks and threats to personal safety
- extreme emotional trauma

These experiences happen spontaneously; one cannot deliberately plan them. The glimpse of the afterlife and its heavenly scenes is so joyous and so elevating that most people who experience it, it seems, do not want to return to their physical bodies. A number of them describe an internal "debate" in which the pull of this attractive alternative is weighed against the desire to "finish" things or be present at a specific event "back on earth."

KARMA

The word *karma* is derived from the sanskrit *kri*, meaning "to do." *Karma*, therefore, is all "doing" or "action." It is known by many other names and phrases, as well: "cause and effect," "law of compensation," "reward and punishment," "law of equilibrium," and even "justice." It is not a very complicated concept; it simply means that whatever we give out, we get back: If we do good, good will come to us; if we do bad, we get bad in return.

Those who have been wronged generally want to see others suffer for their wrong acts. What the wronged person doesn't realize is that, by sending *love* instead of negative feelings to the other individual, there will be a speeding up of the retribution process. The karmic forces are quickened through prayer, praise, love, and light. By sending these *positive* energies, whatever the wrongful person needs to learn (love, kindness, consideration, honesty, etc.), will be learned more quickly. This is the reasoning behind Jesus' admonition to love those who harm us and to turn the other cheek: If we do so, that person will be required to pay back his karmic debt faster.

Sometimes, there is a delay in the lessons administered by the Higher Intelligence and good things continue to be showered upon those who do wrong. But eventually the scales will balance, and payment will be rendered.

You may know (or be!) someone who has a heart of gold yet seems to encounter problems of great magnitude. It is very difficult to understand why one person is born into a life of hardship and another seems to be born with a golden spoon in his mouth. It doesn't seem fair. The answer to the question, "Why does this good person have so many problems?" may never be fully revealed here on earth, but remember that there always is a reason, and usually a valuable lesson, to be learned from such circumstances. (Rabbi Harold Kushner's excellent book, *When Bad Things Happen to Good People,* about his own family experience, is a sensitive exposition of this theory.) Not knowing a person's past life—if past lives exist—we do not know what *karmic debt* he or she may be paying in this life. (Karma exists, in this life, on a daily basis.) But in these circumstances, liberal use of the Law of Praise would greatly help speed up the lessons to be learned.

Those who die young are considered to have paid their karmic debts more quickly than do most of us, hence their shorter than usual life.

THE NATURE OF THE SOUL

The payment of *karmic* debts concerns the transformation of the soul, not the physical body. Your body is the temple of your soul, and so it should be kept in optimum condition, but it is the soul itself that is of supreme importance. The soul is formless, spaceless, and timeless. Although it exists in a different dimension from man's solid, physical body, the soul nevertheless grows and matures with us.

It cannot be destroyed, only transformed into a higher state. In other words, this is the part of our existence that is immortal.

COMMUNICATING WITH DEPARTED SOULS

It is possible to communicate with loved ones who have passed on, and they can communicate with you. The best time to communicate is when you are in a relaxed, meditative state. Concentrate on contacting loved ones by talking with them the way you would talk with a friend. Getting the chills (goose bumps), feeling suddenly hot, hearing a click or a tap in the room, actually hearing a voice, or just getting a strong impression indicates a response. But even if you have no noticeable response, you still may be making contact—and vice versa. Just as in developing your psychic potential, it takes time.

My mother and I had a pact that, whichever of us died first would communicate with the other. She was psychic to an advanced degree—clairaudient, as I am, and clairvoyant. When she was ill in the hospital, I reminded her, "If you don't make it, remember to contact me." She assured me she would. Two weeks later, she died. I was with her at the time and felt her spirit leave her body. Later, crying with my family, I heard my mother's voice say clearly and distinctly, "Linda, I told you I would talk with you. I know you miss me, and I miss all of you, but it's so beautiful here—the mountains, the valleys, the pink and blue flowers. I'm so happy here. I'm with your father and my family. I can help you so much more from here than I could there, and I'll continue to talk to you and help you." And she has.

My mother asked that the following poems be passed out for people to remember her by and to assist others in making the transition, now or in the future:

IMMORTALITY

Do not stand at my grave and weep
I am not there, I do not sleep.
I am a thousand winds that blow,
I am the diamond glints on snow.
I am the sunlight on ripened grain,
I am the gentle autumn's rain.
When you awaken in the morning's hush,
I am the swift uplifting rush.
Of quiet birds in circled flight.
I am the soft star that shined at night.
Do not stand at my grave and cry.
I am not there; I did not die.

—AUTHOR UNKNOWN

BEYOND

When Someone we love has died,
the familiar form been laid aside,
they are not lost, but near at hand
on a higher octave, a wider band
of living light, still true and fond,
a thought away, a step beyond.

—R. H. GRENVILLE

Another story with a similar pact ("whoever dies first . . .") had a different, but just as striking, ending. Sir Laurens van der Post, the South African writer, recounts a story told to him by Carl Jung, in which it was the American philosopher William James and his friend

Dr. Hyslop (later a colleague of the famous Dr. J. B. Rhine, of the Department of Parapsychology at Duke University) who made the pact. When James died and Hyslop heard nothing more from his friend, Hyslop despaired of further investigating communication "through the veil." But seven or eight years later, he received an unexpected letter from a man in Ireland, who—after first apologizing for "bothering" him—explained that he and his wife, using their *Ouija* board, kept getting a message for him from a "very insistent" man named James, who even provided Hyslop's address. In fact, the man confessed, they had been receiving this insistent message for him for the past seven or eight years, but had ignored it—thinking it too unlikely to be valid and fearful of annoying the busy doctor. The message from James was, simply, "Remember the red pajamas." As this referred to an incident about which no one else could have known, Hyslop was certain his deceased friend had sent the communication. The complete story may be found in van der Post's autobiographical *A Walk with a White Bushman* (pp. 152–53).

HOW TO COMMUNICATE WITH YOUR LOVED ONES
WHO HAVE PASSED ON

First, you must realize that your loved ones are not in their physical bodies any longer. Upon physical death, the spiritual body detaches itself and moves quickly into the next dimension. Our loved ones remain close to us, but they are now free of any physical limitations. With the assistance of their "light" beings—their guardian angels and spirit guides—they will work to help those they love with the energy and power available to them. They pray for us and we should pray for them.

Use the same process as for communicating with your guardian angels, only this time incorporate the loved one(s) in your thoughts.

Remember that they are not with you all the time. They, like the spirit guides, have things to do on the other side, as they continue to evolve spiritually, and they can be in only one place at a time. Sometimes, messages will be conveyed to you through their own guardian angels, or through yours. As they evolve into the next dimension and become more and more spiritualized, their appearance will become more and more brilliant. If you ask, they will give you a sign: You will feel their presence, get the chill, hear their voice, the clicks or tapping sounds, or—in some cases—hear from them through "automatic writing" (a phenomenon in which the hand of the "receiver"—involuntarily—begins to write and takes down a message from the other side. A number of famous books have been written this way.)

Don't get discouraged if your loved ones don't communicate with you as quickly as you would like. It takes time for the Higher Forces to arrange all this between the two worlds and you, also, need to be ready. Read, study, meditate, pray, learn, and grow spiritually, to prepare yourself.

As opposed to our guardian angels, who are with us at all times, our loved ones are "angelic assistants" who help us and others as they evolve spiritually. Because they are evolving, they are limited, in varying degrees, in their power to help us. It all depends on their achieved level of spiritual evolvement on the earth plane before their transition.

REINCARNATION

Reincarnation means "reborn in another body." This other body may be physical or spiritual. Most religions, though using different terms ("life after death" or "eternal life"), believe in reincarnation. A belief in a Higher Intelligence is built into the concept of religion along with the idea that a soul does not just end at the time of physical death.

The idea of reincarnation seems to be affirmed by Jesus in Matthew 17:12–13: "But I say unto you, that Elias [Elijah] is come already, and they knew him not. . . . Then the disciples understood that he spoke to them of John the Baptist."

In his second book on past-life therapy, *Through Time into Healing*, psychiatrist Dr. Brian Weiss explains how references to reincarnation were deleted from Christianity and Judaism: "When I researched the history of Christianity, I discovered that early references to reincarnation in the New Testament had been deleted in the fourth century by Emperor Constantine, when Christianity became the official religion of the Roman Empire. Apparently, the emperor had felt that the concept of reincarnation was threatening to the stability of the empire. Citizens who believed they would have another chance to live might be less obedient and law abiding than those who believed in a single Judgment Day for all. In the sixth century, the Second Council of Constantinople underscored Constantine's act by officially declaring reincarnation a heresy."

"In Judaism," Weiss continues, "a fundamental belief in reincarnation, or *gilgul*, has existed for thousands of years. This belief had been a basic cornerstone of the Jewish faith until approximately 1800–1850, when the urge to modernize and to be accepted by the more scientific Western establishment transformed the Eastern European Jewish communities. . . . In the Orthodox and Hasidic communities, belief in reincarnation continues unabated today. The Kabbala, mystical Jewish literature dating back thousands of years, is filled with references to reincarnation."

Buddhists, along with the followers of other Eastern religions, believe that each of us is in an eternal earthly reincarnation, determined by how well we abide by God's laws during each lifetime. If we do well and become enlightened during this lifetime, we should return to a better existence in the next earthly life; if we are evil, we would probably return on a much lower level. In this way, we pay for our earthly sins and eventually become one with God.

Today, there are many reasons people believe in reincarnation, not the least of which is that it makes the fact of "death" easier to accept. (This actually may have more to do with an ability to communicate with the deceased than a belief in future lives, but they are closely related.)

One of the most interesting answers given to the question, "Why do you believe in reincarnation?" is "Mozart." The person responding in that way went on to explain that there seems no other explanation for a two-year-old child's ability to climb onto a piano bench and play perfect music, never having had the first lesson: He must have been an "old soul." Others explain their belief by saying it just doesn't make sense that people would spend their lives amassing information and experience, only to die and have it all disappear. Perhaps the most compelling reason is the often-experienced sense of *déjà vu*, which makes people certain they have been somewhere or seen something before—even while knowing that to be an impossibility (in this lifetime!). Television programs and books describing people with knowledge simply unavailable to them in their present life show how common an experience this is and lend credence to a belief that these people have, indeed, lived before. When the book *The Search for Bridey Murphy* came out in the 1950s—one of the first to popularize the notion that we *all* have lived before—the medical community was so scandalized, they declared it a fraud. The author later supposedly confessed it was fiction, but researchers who attested to verifying the validity of other similar incidents never believed the confession. Today, the book would be just one of a vast number expressing similar beliefs.

When people come to me for past-lifetime readings, I receive information on these past lives psychically. One can relive such lives through a hypnotic process called "regression training." It is well documented—by the American Society of Psychical Research, among others—that people have dreams, visions, and other variously detailed experiences relating to the past that they have no way of knowing in this lifetime. Yet, as I evolved more, I began to question the source of this information. Continuing my research, I came across the writings of Carl Jung and his theory of "the collective unconscious."

Jung, in his *Modern Man in Search of a Soul*, says, "My unconscious mind stretches far out of this environment, backwards in time. . . . Just as man has the whole development of mankind in his body . . . gills in his neck, for instance, that go back to the fishes . . . so every man has the whole history of the world in his unconscious mind." This astounding statement implies that, since each man has had literally millions of human ancestors who have lived in every habitable area of the globe, his ancestral memory includes all the experiences of every one of those ancestors.

Incredibly, as iconoclastic an idea as this was at the time, the American writer Jack London, in a short story called "Before Adam," advanced the almost identical theory, publishing half a world away but at practically the same time as Jung.

The evidence of heredity shows that ancestral memory, like all other characteristics, is transmitted through the genes of the father's sperm cell and the mother's egg cell. Thus, every newborn creature, human or otherwise, has the ancestral memories of two parents, four grandparents, eight great-grandparents, and so on, back through the centuries.

It is possible to develop ancestral memory through the various meditation, visualization, and mental programming techniques outlined in this book. You need not be hypnotized, nor possessed of the powers of a "medium" to make use of this memory. As I told a young man about to take an exam in Russian language (knowing he had two Russian great-grandfathers), "When you're stuck for an answer, just tap into your collective unconscious and get the answer from your relatives"!

Whether the information I receive during a past-lifetime reading, is the actual past life of the person himself, or that of his ancestor, I believe it to be valid in some way. But I do not dwell on my own past lives: I just ask God to forgive me for any injustices I may have committed and allow me to live my life now, to the highest and best it can be.

A person's having been good or bad, during his earthly life will not change the fact that his soul continues on, but a person who violates God's laws while on earth will take longer to progress down the path of enlightenment. Man creates his destiny with his mind; his choices here on earth affect the extent he will progress.

Many believe that recalling past lives—through any number of techniques—can explain much about your present life, including physical and emotional problems. Dr. Weiss explains that "past life regression is expanding the repertoire of known techniques for accessing what has recently been dubbed 'the mind-body connection.'" He continues by noting that "past life therapy is particularly effective in treating musculoskeletal pain, headaches that do not respond to medication, allergies, asthma, and stress-induced or immune system–related conditions. . . . It also resolves deep, underlying emotional issues, as the relationship of the emotions to the physical discomfort and its past life source is revealed."

What an extraordinary statement to be taken so for granted, today, when we reflect on the fact that, not that many years ago, this same Dr. Weiss—in his first book on the subject, *Many Lives, Many Masters*—confessed it took him four years to decide to *write* the book, so certain was he that he would be "run out of the profession" by his colleagues for such apostasy. Never for a moment, he tells us, did he anticipate the flood of mail he received, from others in his field, who had theretofore been equally nervous about discussing their (similar) findings in this area.

HOW TO HAVE A PAST LIFE RECALL

1. Be open and receptive to feelings and perceptions in meditations, guided visualizations and mind exercises. A past-life memory may be triggered by a present situation which is similar to a past experience. You may have a sense or a feeling about the memories without seeing them clearly in your mind's eye. You may become aware of a past-life connection, symbols, or images without knowing exactly what the connection is.
2. Consulting a qualified hypnotherapist, knowledgeable in past-life regressions, is advisable.
3. To open up past-life memories you must learn to consciously relax—completely—so that your subconscious becomes more aware.
4. Follow the meditation techniques—the mental, spiritual, and physical preparations to meditate. You can also incorporate the rainbow meditation of breathing, bathing, and absorbing each color.
5. Call upon the higher forces and spiritual beings/angels to assist you.
6. When past memories come to you, pay attention to details: your mode of dress, the landscape, the weather, the people, noises, smells, conversations, even whether you are male or female, child or adult.

7. Trust your intuition, to help open your past life recall to a greater extent and to provide you with even more information. When you pay attention to your intuition, you are in touch with your subconscious.

8. Your imagination is a powerful resource. Use it to dream about the possibilities of what you might have been and what you might have done in a past life. Let inspiration guide you.

9. Choose a situation in your life that is troubling you, or one that seems unfair. Ask yourself what you did to deserve it. Be honest with yourself. Let go of preconceived thoughts and let flow the images, thoughts, and feelings of all the possibilities and probabilities of what you may have done or experienced in a past life.

10. Keep a journal. Meditate, as you go, on the interpretations—to analyze pictures, impressions, and ideas.

FREE WILL AND PREDESTINATION—MY OWN BELIEFS

For about seven years, I firmly believed in the classic Eastern (Hindu) theory on reincarnation. I studied the teachings of people like Arthur Ford, Edgar Cayce, Gina Cerminara, Ruth Montgomery, Vera Stanley Adler, Jiddu Krishnamurti, Peter Ouspensky, Yogi Ramacharaka, Djwal Khul, Parmahansa Yohananda's Self Realization Fellowship, and various swamis and yogis with the same basic concept. Reincarnation seemed to answer the questions regarding why we were born into our particular life situation, good or bad.

I no longer believe in this classic theory. I now feel that, when we die after our life on earth, we do not return here. If that were the case, life on earth would never fully evolve; we could never repay all our karmic debts, no matter how many lives we lived.

Rather than dwell on or ponder this subject, I prefer to deal with the here and now. What is important to me—and, indeed, what seems important to *most* people—is life and its problems and potential as *presently* experienced. Love, health, jobs, money: These are our overwhelming concerns.

Having said that, let me hasten to add that I have no quarrel with those who believe in and study the possibilities of reincarnation. But they have no proof. (Are we tapping into a past life or into Jung's collective unconscious?) As an open-minded person, I am certainly interested in the various theories, but my own clients, viewers, and readers are better served by me by being helped to deal with *this* lifetime.

I believe our physical bodies are recycled on earth, while our souls—developed through our various experiences and the choices we made here—survive. Our personalities, which are our identifying factors, also survive death. After death, there is a waiting period that may last millions of years but will seem as nothing, since all sense of time will be gone. Then, in an instant, we will be reincarnated into a place that Jesus refers to as "mansions." These are places where our souls rest for a time, and where they are educated and cleansed by spirits and angels before ascending to higher spiritual planes. In the mansion worlds, we do not have physical bodies, but we certainly are aware of our existence. Our spiritual body is a luminous likeness of our physical body during its prime of life. Even if you were sick during that time, your spiritual body in the next dimension will be in optimum condition. There is no disease. You may choose what you want to look like: tall or short, thin or heavy, blond or brunette. Your mind will make any change you want. Others will recognize you not by your body but by your personality.

In this mansion world we have shelter and learn in large classes similar to lecture halls. We have free will but also are governed by laws. There is perfect justice and everyone is accountable for his actions. Unlike on earth, here we are separated on different levels by vibrations: Those of similar vibrations will share the same level. We see and are assisted by our close loved ones and by our guardian angels. From the mansion worlds we are incarnated into other planes of existence until we finally become one with God. That is the final incarnation for all of us.

These concepts are based on information in the *Urantia Book*, which a good friend gave me about fifteen years ago. It details the life and teachings of Jesus, delves into the history of the planet Earth, and explains the operations of this and other universes.

Although I was raised a Catholic, believing that Jesus was the son of God and that all their religious rituals were necessary to reach heaven, I have evolved to the point that I now consider myself a nondenominational Christian. I still believe that Jesus is the son of God, but I believe in harmony among religions. The Eastern religions I studied teach that Jesus was just another prophet, along with Mohammed, Confucius, Moses, and Buddha. But even then, whenever I meditated, I would concentrate on Jesus' energy surrounding me, because I always felt most comfortable with him. That, however, does not change my belief that God resides in all churches and temples, all homes and hearts.

While I enjoy going into churches and temples, I do not feel it necessary to go on any particular day or to any particular place, in order to communicate with God. Rather, I pray daily from my "inner temple." Even Jesus expressed this thought: "The time is coming . . . when we will no longer be concerned about whether to worship the Father here or in Jerusalem. For it is not where we worship that counts, but how we worship—is our worship spiritual and real?" (John 4:21).

Nor do I believe that baptisms, confessions, or taking communion are necessary. To me, these are just ceremonies—beautiful and moving as they may be. I recognize that some people feel more psychologically and spiritually committed, performing an act to prove the commitment they feel, but I don't think ceremonies necessarily have anything to do with moving closer to God—which is my only religious concern. Likewise, some feel it necessary to communicate through an intermediary who has dedicated his life to God, believing it brings them closer to Him, but I don't believe people have to climb onto a stage or pulpit with a minister to rededicate their lives in order to be born again. These practices have been a necessity for other people, however, and in many cases they may truly have saved their lives.

Many also believe that, in order to be "saved" you must accept Jesus as your Savior and your only means of entering Heaven. I feel you can get to know God better by going directly to the source: through meditation, prayer, and service. The real importance of Jesus lies in what He did during His life, not in His death. Jesus didn't come to earth to save us but, rather, to teach us how to save ourselves and to teach us of the Fatherhood of God and the brotherhood of man. He, like Moses, taught the Father's Will. In other words, the golden rule of loving one another by demonstrating it.

To those who believe in Jesus' Second Coming, I say that I feel His return will be not in human form but as a spiritual awakening and a Christ-realization of His principles within each and every one of us, within our own hearts and souls. It is disturbing to see people who profess to be Christians leading lives quite far from what Jesus taught, sometimes engaging even in criminal behavior. They believe that because Jesus is their Savior, they can go on leading a negative life and that, no matter what they do, Jesus will save them in the end. Naturally, I do not agree.

Religion is something we work on individually, through a con-

scious spiritual awakening and through making a personal commitment. Anything that helps us to become better people and move
closer to God is fine with me. We don't have to discuss our religious
beliefs with anyone else, and certainly it is not necessary to get up in
front of a roomful of people to demonstrate sincerity. Religion is between you and God. You alone decide the way that is best for you.

As I have said earlier in this book, my concept of God is that
of a Higher Power, a vibrating sea of intellectual energy, cosmic
power, Infinite Intelligence—omniscient, omnipresent, omnipotent.
We are made of cosmic energy created by this Central Source, energy which cannot be used up but can be recycled into another form.
If you evolve spiritually while here on earth, it will be easier to make
the transition through physical death into these wonderful new
planes of existence.

Although my beliefs lean more toward Christianity than to
any other religion, no one religion is perfect or has all the answers.
Depend upon your own feelings and the divine guidance you receive.
Then make your own decision about what is right for you, knowing
that—as you become closer to God—you will come closer to the realization of your highest and greatest potential.

Chapter Two

PSYCHIC PHENOMENA AND DEVELOPMENT

VIBRATIONS

To understand where your psychic feelings come from, it helps to understand something about vibrations. The term *vibrations* (sometimes called "vibes"), was often used in the 1960s (my generation) as a catch-all phrase to describe a feeling or impression you get from another person, from situations, or even from locations. For example, if you said, "I get bad vibes from him," you meant you didn't trust the person in question. It may be easy to "write off" this term as just another sixties fad or "buzzword," but, in fact, we do get such vibrations from people, places, and things, and these vibrations can be measured scientifically.

One of the major areas of scientific research, in recent decades, has been that surrounding the *atom* and its potential and role in life. The atomic bomb is an example of how scientists were able to turn the atom's vibrations into a powerful destructive force. On a more positive note, the atom has been found to be the basic element of all things found in our universe. The difference between living and nonliving and between gases and solids is simply a difference in atomic vibration. Our senses may tell us, when we touch a chair, that it is solid, but actually it is a field of electronic and protonic energies moving at a set rate of vibration.

The whole world, we discover, is in a state of ever-becoming. There is never a rest in this atomic movement; all matter is in a constant state of change, whether we can perceive it with the naked eye or not. For this reason, scientific theory now holds that the universe is not a *thing*, but, rather, a *series of processes*. Because process is difficult for us to *see* (we tend to think "seeing is believing"), our perception of the world remains inherently distorted.

Throughout history, people who had unusually high intuitive or ESP (extrasensory perception) ability have claimed they weren't limited in time or space, that they could see into the future as well as into the past. In fact, they had learned to detect and interpret the atomic vibrations and to move knowingly within the seen and unseen worlds of existence.

The ancient sages understood the importance of these vibrations. It is interesting to note that, although their fact-finding methods differed greatly from today's *scientific* method, many of the conclusions reached then were essentially the same as those scientists are reporting today. While no one has yet discovered what the force is that causes atoms to vibrate, we do know that atoms differ from one another according to their rates of vibration and according to the number and action of the minute particles called *protons* and *neutrons* that form the atom's nucleus. Vibration makes the atoms move out in all directions, bombarding other surrounding atoms. These collisions have a measured effect on, but do not destroy, the individual atoms.

A favorite illustration scientists use to explain this phenomenon shows someone throwing a stone into a still pond. When the stone strikes the surface, it sends out ripples in all directions, at a rate proportional to the force of the stone's hitting the water. If several stones are thrown into the pond, the emanating ripples move out from each stone's point of entry, sometimes overlapping other ripples but not destroying them. The distance between ripples is called the "wavelength." This illustration serves also to describe what happens when waves of light, sound, heat, or even *thought* disturb the atmosphere.

To give you an idea of the wide range of vibration rates, solids send out waves of disturbance at a rate under sixteen vibrations per second (vps) while light and color are at 500 *billion*. The *vps* rate of etheric, astral, mental, and spiritual vibrations is, as yet, unknown.

Although, with our five senses, we are able to perceive only a very small range of vibrations, a great deal of evidence indicates that, through development of other latent senses, we can go much further in our exploration of vibrations. (Consider how often you hear someone refer to having "a sixth sense" about something, indicating an intuitive feeling.)

The highest vibrations use the ether as their mode of travel. The ether (not to be confused with the anesthetic) is the substance that holds all atoms in place. These highest of vibrations are within reach of the human mind and are termed *psychic vibrations*. The *aura*, or energy field surrounding all living things, is also part of the ether.

The pituitary and the pineal gland (located toward the front of the brain, roughly between the eyebrows, and often called "the third eye") are thought to play a great part in the opening of the psychic channel. Apparently, these two organs—about which rather little is known—are sensitive to psychic vibrations. If they are properly stimulated, they act as translators of these higher vibrations. (Do you touch your forehead when you're trying to concentrate on something or figure out an answer?) Some people are born with an inherent ability to see the finer magnetic or electrical vibrations going on in the ether, vibrations that make up another entire world of thought forms, entities, and their activities. These supersensitive people are known as *clairvoyants*.

Though little is known about how the pineal and pituitary glands receive and interpret these higher vibrations, more has been learned in recent years about how the brain works. I have talked about how positive thinking (i.e., sending out positive vibrations) can affect your life. Let's look now at some of the physiological proof behind these theories, which directly relate to the brain's functioning.

The human brain produces electrical activity that can be picked up and measured by use of an EEG (electroencephalograph), using electrodes attached to the scalp. Several patterns can be identified, such as the predominant *beta* frequency, at 14–21 cycles per second. The *beta* waves are associated with the fully-awake state, characterized by the ability to control physical ideas and concepts and to function logically. The *alpha* rhythm, at 7–14 cycles per second, is the relaxed, creative, intuitive state. The *alpha* waves come into play when we are developing our ESP ability, through sleep therapy and meditation. In meditation or light sleep, the brain usually operates on the *alpha* level. (This is the level those who use *Silva Mind Control*—now known as *the Silva Method*—work to develop. In the early years, its adherents used the phrase "go to *alpha*" as a shorthand way of saying, "use your intuitive state.") The *theta* level, 4–7 cycles per second, is associated with deep sleep or total unconsciousness.

It is well known and often lamented that we use only about 10 percent of our brain's potential in our daily lives. What about the other 90 percent or more? The answer to developing our latent psychic abilities lies in the large portion of the brain. Obviously, the potential is tremendous. The person who learns to control his brain waves will be able to shift awareness *at will* to that part of the mind where the *psi* factor—that so-called "extra" or "sixth" sense—operates, a sense *each and every one of us* has the capacity to develop.

MEASURING BRAIN WAVES

I have spoken about the energy each thought possesses and how thoughts are tangible things that have a direct effect on our world. There is also evidence that the energy released by our thoughts has some degree of *staying power*. Dr. Oscar Brunler, an expert on brain radiations, espouses the following theory:

> Besides measuring the radiation of the brain directly from the head, we can measure it from a person's signature, from his handwriting, from his paintings and drawings. The eyes which are watching the letters as they are written down radiate a force on the paper or on the canvas on which we paint. We can measure the radiation from the handwriting and check it up with the writer's brain radiation, and we find that both are identical. It is possible to measure, even after centuries, the brain radiations of people. As an example, the radiations of the paintings of Leonardo da Vinci, the greatest all-round genius the world has known, and the manuscripts of this great man, give the identical wave-length, and his is the highest radiation I have discovered so far, namely 725 degrees Biometric, which corresponds to a wave-length shorter than the shortest invisible ultra-violet rays.

Thus, since our brain radiations are within our power to control, it follows logically that we possess the ability to raise our intellect and our spiritual aspirations.

RIGHT-BRAIN AND LEFT-BRAIN THINKING

To begin our study of how better to control our brain waves, let us start with the standard intelligence test and its limitations. The standard I.Q., or Intelligence Quotient, tests—widely used to measure intellect—test only the left, or reasoning side, of the brain. The right side of the brain, which controls nonverbal intelligence, creativity, and intuition, is ignored. Throughout history, there have been people who were considered brilliant who, it turns out, did poorly in school. Winston Churchill, Albert Einstein, and Thomas Edison are three prime examples. It may very well be that they did poorly *in school* because they were right-brain oriented.

The right brain operates differently from the "logical" left brain. In the right brain, an idea usually incubates in the subconscious for several days—or even months or years—before it surfaces. After this period of incubation—when the time (thought?) is "ripe"—it might just pop into your head ("Eureka!") without your consciously having summoned it. Don't ever discard such thoughts: They come from the right, or intuitive side, of the brain and should be given careful consideration. Your right brain is always trying, through such thoughts, intuition, feelings, and sometimes even dreams, to communicate its messages to you. Most people ignore such occurrences, dismissing them as "just a hunch." But creative people call it *inspiration* and know to follow their intuition. In this way, they find solutions to complicated problems amazingly quickly, because they cut through all the left-brain reasoning and get right to the answer.

Certain types of people are unquestionably more receptive to right-brain thinking. Research suggests that those who are open-minded, sensitive, and unbiased are far more likely to experience this intuition, or ESP. Those who are withdrawn, depressed, worried, and negative are, generally, unreceptive to ESP. This doesn't mean they cannot experience it, just that their underlying fear and mistrust block the flow of transmission (hence, the expression, "be *open* to it").

In achieving our goals of sensing and using these right-brain vibrations, the holistic concept cannot be overemphasized. In fact, you will never be able to get in touch with these vibrations if your body and mind are full of unstable, unhealthy, inharmonious, and conflicting vibrations. To reach this goal you must first be as strong and as calm as possible in spirit, mind, and body.

EXTRASENSORY PERCEPTION

There are many different ways, physical and mental, in which we receive spiritual and psychic information. The spiritual sciences deal with an inner awareness in which there is spiritual communication (often called "psychic ability"). This takes place in a number of ways:

APPORTS: The rare psychic power by which material objects are brought into being by supernormal means—materializing from another dimension, from one place to another in this dimension, or from spirit. For example, an important letter is left in a wall safe, but appears on the table without assistance.

ASTRAL PROJECTION: When the astral, or spiritual, body leaves the physical body, usually when you are in an altered state. It can travel on the earth plane or in other dimensions, and then return to the physical body.

AURA READING: Seeing or feeling the colors of someone's aura, and interpreting them.

AUTOMATIC SPEAKING: The power wherein the psychic person speaks or even sings in another person's voice. This is also known as *glossolalia* or "speaking in tongues." The psychic may even speak in a language he or she doesn't know consciously. A group of psychic development students, for example, are meditating, when suddenly one of them begins speaking with a different voice. The voice tells another student that he need not worry about his aunt, who will be fine. The voice leaves as suddenly as it came.

AUTOMATIC WRITING: The ability to write physically through contact with the Divine Intelligence or one of His angelic representatives. A spiritual force comes through the hand and writes without effort on the part of the author. Many authors have this divine assistance. If you are thinking, for example, about an upcoming court case as you unconsciously doodle on paper, you may look down and see the words, "Everything will be O.K."

CHANNELING: A *medium* is a person who can tap into the spirit world and receive messages. The so-called New Age term for medium is *channeler*. Hundreds of channelers have popped up nationwide. Of all those who claim to be channelers, a certain percentage are fraudulent and take advantage of people emotionally and financially. Even among those who can truly channel, no one is 100 percent accurate. Most come up with very general, universal spiritual messages. A true channeler will be able to come up with specific information as well. Everyone, in a sense, can channel information. It can be as simple as receiving an answer from God, or the Higher Being. Some channelers "leave" their bodies and let another entity take over. The channeler goes into a light trance and the energy of the entity, or spirit, enters the channeler and speaks through him.

CLAIRAUDIENCE: The power to hear sounds (not in the usual physical sense) of a paranormal nature. The word means "clear-hearing." A woman and her son, Jerry, had been extremely close; he had called her faithfully every night until the day he was killed in an automobile accident. Months later, overcome with grief, she cried, "Why don't you call me anymore?" At that moment, the phone rang. When she answered it, the voice on the other end said, "Mom . . ." She recognized the voice of her son and said, "Jerry!" The voice repeated, "Mom . . ." and then just drifted away. She went into the bedroom, where her husband asked who was on the phone. She said it was Jerry. Her husband, puzzled, said, "It must have been someone who sounded like him." "No," she said. "I know his voice. He called me and then just drifted away."

Hearing clairaudiently can sound like a whispering voice in your head. Although the voice's volume varies slightly, it is always more quiet than a normal voice and often can be heard on just one side.

CLAIRSAVORANCE: The power to perceive flavors in the paranormal sense, when the source of that flavor is not physically present.

CLAIRSENSUOUSNESS: The power to feel various sensory phenomena in a supernormal manner. There are four types: tactile, thermal, kinesthetic, and pain-and-pleasure. For example, while speaking with a particular person, you have pain in the joints of your hand, which lasts briefly—until you learn that the person has arthritic pain in the hands.

CLAIRSENTIENCE: The power to perceive smells of a paranormal nature, but not in the physical sense. For example, perceiving a burning smell when there is nothing burning nearby, then learning that your friend's house burned down. Another example would be if you smell your mother's favorite perfume around you, when there is no evidence of it nearby. You could be sensing her spirit near you.

CLAIRVOYANCE: The power to perceive or "see" (not with the physical eye) visions of a paranormal nature (not within the range of normal experience; not scientifically explainable). The word means "clear-seeing." There are various forms of clairvoyance, such as *mediumistic* (seeing visions and auras shown to us by the Divine Intelligence and His angelic representatives in the other dimension), and *projected* (seeing distant objects and places). For example, you could be talking on the phone as you get a flash of yourself sitting on a white sandy beach, tropical drink in hand. Later, you learn you have won a trip to Hawaii.

DOWSING: A method of locating an energy source by using a device like a forked stick, L-rod, or pendulum. Through the subconscious or superconscious mind, dowsing relies on feelings, mind energy, motion, and gravity. For instance, you buy some land and want to determine the best place to build a well. Using a dowsing stick, you follow the direction the stick's point takes you.

IMPRESSIONALISM: The power to perceive ideas imposed by the God-force through His spiritual representative.

These impressions, which are limitless in scope, are typically ideas that simply come to mind, like a hunch or feeling. For instance, you might be late for work and rushing to get there. You feel you should take a side street on the way, rather than the main thoroughfare. Later, you learn there was a big accident on the street you originally planned to take.

INDEPENDENT SPEAKING: Spiritual beings speaking in an audible voice from out of nowhere or from an animate or inanimate object. Many people have been on the verge of falling asleep while driving, when a voice from nowhere said, very loudly, "Wake up!" Richard Bach said he received information for his inspirational book *Jonathan Livingston Seagull,* from a gull that appeared to him in a vision and verbally dictated the story to him.

MATERIALIZATION: The rare power in which seemingly physical objects are created. A spiritual form physically appears and can easily be seen by others. There are many examples in the Bible, including one where angels appeared and moved the stone covering Jesus' tomb. A materialization requires a great deal of spiritual energy (ectoplasm) and occurs rarely. However, materialization does not have to be in human form: Objects, too, may materialize, like a ring appearing on a dressing room table out of nowhere.

PARA-EMOTIONALISM: The power to feel various emotional states imposed supernormally by external personalities. For example, a psychic could pick up the feeling or vibration of a client's brother because of the emotion of "brotherly love." The psychic could then relay the feeling, and the brother's message, to the client.

PSYCHIC DREAMS: The power to gather information from psychic sources while in the sleeping state. Not all dreams are psychic ones—only those which tell a truth, the future, or information that otherwise would be unavailable to the person receiving it. This information is later confirmed by actual events. For instance, a client, Sue, related this story: One morning, her sister was distraught because she had misplaced her wedding pictures. Sue meditated on her sister's problem all day and before bed prayed that an answer be revealed in her sleep. During the night, she dreamed that the wedding photos had slid under the seat of her sister's car. The next morning, when she awoke, Sue called her sister with the information. Her sister went out to her car, where she found the photos under the seat.

PSYCHIC RAPS: This is a form of code system between our world and the "other" world. The sounds, which can be heard with the physical ear, include snapping, knocking, cracking, even scratching. A person familiar with such means of communication would notice these raps and interpret them as confirmation of whatever he or she was thinking at the time.

PSYCHOMETRY: The ability to pick up an object and sense its history or origin and certain other factors about it. For example, a psychic might pick up a set of keys belonging to another person and be able to describe that person in detail—including where the person is and what he or she is feeling. The impressions can be felt as ideas and emotions, in the psychic sense. In the case of missing persons, psychics frequently are hired by the police to locate or describe victims and/or crime suspects. Vibrations are actually picked up from the object belonging—or having belonged—to the subject. Psychometry is always associated with inanimate objects, never living things.

SEERSHIP: The power to know about distant happenings or places in a paranormal manner. For example, the seer may see, hear, feel, or even smell something that represents what is happening somewhere else or in the future. The seer may have a vision of a group of miners trapped in a coal mine in England, then—a week later—hear a report on the news that it is happening.

TELEKINESIS: The power that moves objects without physical contact. Objects can move, rise, or float in the air. For example, I have witnessed Olof Jonsson, using his own mind power, make a candlestick glide across a table without touching it.

TELEPATHY: The power to send or receive thoughts and emotions—in other words, to read another person's thought vibrations. For example, you send a friend to the store with a shopping list but realize you forgot to include butter. You send mental messages to your friend, who returns with the butter, saying he had the feeling you needed it, even though it wasn't on the list.

TRANCE: A state of consciousness reached through meditation. Information is received from the spirit world through the subconscious mind of the psychic/ medium who is in the trance state. An example of such a person is Edgar Cayce, who was called "the Sleeping Prophet," and who could diagnose illnesses—with no medical training—by the use of information gleaned while in a trance state.

SIGNS OF ESP AWAKENING

Most of the conditions and abilities described in the previous section are first felt as signs of development. Some signs frequently noticed by those developing an ESP ability are reduced or accelerated heart action; a sinking, spinning, or rising feeling; excessive perspiration; nausea; unusual sleepiness; slowing down of breathing; and/or a prickling sensation, especially in the hands, head, and face area.

An endless variety of supernormal signs may go with a number of psychic abilities, ranging from simple changes in physical condition to complex alterations in one's psychological makeup. Here are some examples:

CLAIRVOYANCE: Burning irritation of the eyes; seeing lights (various sizes and colors)

CLAIRAUDIENCE: Itching sensations within the ear; buzzing, tinkling sounds; perception of whispering voices; musical sounds difficult to describe

CLAIRSENTIENCE: Irritations or tickling in the nose; perception of odors

CLAIRSENSUOUSNESS: Temperature changes in various parts of the body; feeling of something creepy on the body

CLAIRSAVORANCE: Sensitivity in the tongue (swelling or tenderness); perception of tasting various flavors

IMPRESSIONALISM: Unusual ideas that have relevance coming to mind consistently

INSPIRATION: Pain or pressure in a spot in the center of the forehead; a sensation just above the diaphragm

AUTOMATIC WRITING: Feeling of energy flowing through the hand or arm; coldness, heaviness, or prickling sensations in the hand or arm

AUTOMATIC SPEAKING: Choking, tightening, burning,
    or irritating sensations in the throat or vocal chords
TELEKINESIS: Heaviness, numbness in the body or just
    in the arms or legs; pressure at the base of the brain;
    sensation of something being drawn from the solar
    plexus or natural body openings. Just as no two people
    are alike, no two people will experience ESP develop-
    ment in the same way. One may be more responsive
    to signs that are visual, another to signs that are
    audible, etc.

A word of warning: Refrain from attributing every "strange" or "out of the ordinary" event in your life to developing ESP ability. Most of what happens to you has a physiological base, not a "paranormal" one. In addition, some of the ESP development signs mentioned above, such as ringing in the ears, could, in fact, be related to a developing medical condition. Always check these things out with a physician.

OTHER WAYS OF RECEIVING DIVINE ANSWERS

Some of the psychic abilities mentioned above may be combined with a *learned* psychic science, such as palmistry or tarot card reading, enabling almost anyone to tell certain things about another person or about himself. For instance, a palmist who looks at your hand and tells you that someone named "Joe" will be coming into your life is using his or her *psychic* ability. (There is no way the name is revealed on your hand alone.) But psychic ability is not *necessary* to make use of these mechanical means to know more about the present or forecasting the future. These various means may be learned by anyone willing to take the time. Throughout the ages, individuals have tried to tap into the mysterious forces of the universe in order to divine the future by the use of one or more of the following:

PALMISTRY is the science of reading the lines of the hands to tell where a person has been, where he is going, and what his options are for change. Palmistry is much more than simple "fortune-telling." It is an ancient art much older than recorded time. The hands' lines change as you change, as you face new hardships or triumphs in life. A study of the hand can tell you about your physical and emotional health, your personality, your chances for success in a chosen career, and what it might take to achieve your life's fulfillment in the areas of creativity, love, and spiritual development. Without going into the intricacies of palmistry, which can be learned by reading a number of good books on the subject, remember that the left hand is supposed to show the innate potential with which you were born and the right hand how you have used that potential. Besides studying the lines in the hands, a good palmist will also find clues in the *shape* of a person's hand and in its general appearance.

In spirituality, man represents the microcosm of the universe—the five-pointed star—with the head, two arms, and the legs representing the points. In palmistry, the hand represents this microcosm, with the four fingers and thumb as the five points. Looking at the palm gives valuable insight into a person's life in miniature.

NUMEROLOGY has been around for centuries. Some say it began with the Kabbalists of ancient Egypt; others claim the origin lies with the Greek philosopher

Pythagoras, of the sixth century B.C., known as "the Father of Numbers." In numerology, the letters of names and the numbers of the birthdate are combined to form other numbers that explain and interpret various aspects of a person's life. Numerology is not explained by traditional scientific means; it operates on the universal value of numbers, psychic energy, the vibratory effect of numbers, and the God-force. Knowledge of your number will enable you to better deal with upcoming circumstances. According to numerologists, changing your name can change your destiny. (A number of famous entertainers claim to have used numerology in determining the spelling of their names.)

TAROT CARDS are used to interpret the past, present, and future, and to answer questions, if properly interpreted by someone who fully understands each card's symbols. To say they can completely and accurately predict your future would be to give their powers far too much weight. Often, they provide psychological insight and, like palm reading, can be used to find out more about ourselves. Tarot is much less complicated than astrology, which is a proven and complicated science based on concrete facts and mathematics. The tarot's subtle ancient messages are usually open to more than one interpretation. The origin of tarot has been traced back to the twelfth century. Many scholars believe our ordinary decks of playing cards are directly descended from the tarot.

ASTROLOGY is a three-to-five-thousand-year-old study of the earth's relationship to the universe within a space/time framework. Astrology has been called "the

Psychology of the Ancients." It correlates the earth's events to our planet's positional relationship to other members of the solar system. One of the most common uses of astrology is as a tool for personal advice in all its aspects—relationships, career, business decisions, travel plans, even the best place (country, city) to live. The sun, moon, and all the planets of our solar system, with the exception of the earth, are used as the astrological symbols and represent specific values and qualities.

An astrological chart is divided into twelve equal parts of a circle. Each part, called a "house," covers thirty degrees and represents a specific area of life (i.e., relationships, career, communication, money, etc.). A "birth chart"—the one most frequently used—shows the exact location of each of the planets at the moment and place of your birth. The precise, mathematical, angular relationships of these planets may then be interpreted. This is known as "reading" your chart. It is from a book called an *Ephemerus* that the positions of the planets are taken, so a chart can be done by anyone who has learned to read the *Ephemerus*—or even by computer. But it is the *interpretation* of the relationships that is of greatest importance, once the chart is done, and that takes a great deal of study. The most competent "readers" (astrologers) are those who can add psychic ability to this depth of knowledge, for they are able to draw on their *multiple* talents. Though more rare, they are well worth seeking out. (The most competent among them establish your chart as they speak with you, not requiring an *Ephemerus* at all.) Once the "natal" or "birth" chart is constructed, updated or "progressed" charts—showing the planets in their *present* positions—can be produced and read.

Most often, when people ask you your astrological sign, they are referring to your "sun sign" only—i.e., where the sun was, in your chart, at your moment and place of birth. This is also what you find in newspaper and magazine columns. But while your sun sign is of certain and special importance, the various aspects and influences of *other* celestial bodies also have distinct influence and effect. Some astrologers feel your "rising sign"—representing the first impression you give to others—is of equal or greater importance.

THROWING THE BONES is a form of divination practiced by the witch doctors of Africa. Actually a collection of animal bones, shells, coins, and pieces of ivory or wood, each one representing a specific person or circumstance, these objects are "thrown" onto a straw mat and "read" to describe and diagnose a variety of problems. Witch doctors go through ten years of intensive training and liken themselves to the psychologists and psychiatrists of the West. Two books which describe these practices in detail are *White Woman Witchdoctor* and *African Divination Systems*.

CRYSTALS

Throughout time, man has used precious gems and metals to decorate his body, aid in healing, and perform other practical functions. All crystals contain some degree of metal, the vibrations of which can affect the body. Crystal lenses discovered in ancient ruins are thought to have been used to cauterize wounds. Crystal energy today is found extensively in electronic products: Since crystals amplify and transmit electromagnetic energy, they are used in radios, televisions, and radar, and are unique in their ability to create the microelectronic circuits used in computers.

In choosing a crystal, be aware that, as they differ structurally, they perform different functions. Choose them based on your intuition and attraction to them, as well as for the spiritual and functional purposes you desire.

Some of the most popular crystals and gemstones are:

AMETHYST For inner peace, protection, spiritual attunement. Gives visions and opens spiritual and psychic centers; reduces mental tension; induces pleasant healing dreams; prevents overindulgence and encourages transformation and breaking of bad habits; promotes wisdom and humility; strengthens will power; helps with low self-esteem.

AVENTURINE: For abundance, healing, and spiritual growth; cleanses the etheric, emotional, and mental bodies; alleviates anxiety and buried fears; brings adventures in love life and good luck.

BLUE QUARTZ: Helps alleviate depression; helps with those who are afraid of growing older; increases longevity; enhances one's creative abilities; aligns subtle bodies.

CARNELIAN: Gives a feeling of well-being and an extra boost of energy; good for liver, respiratory system, tender gums. Placed on navel during past life regression or rebirthing helps bring up past experiences; improves sense of touch.

CITRINE: For cheerfulness, control over emotions, clear thought; overcomes mental blocks, aids digestion, brings light force into the physical plane; encourages compassion, mental discipline; helps clear one of depression and self-destructive tendencies (especially suicide). This is a cheerful and happy stone, bringing one all the best things in life; good for stomach, intestines, kidneys, liver, muscle, and for removing wastes and toxins from the blood.

HEMATITE: The circulation stone, good for blood disorders and burns, as it heals dangerous wounds. Good for lungs, spine, low vitality, headaches, high blood pressure, hemorrhages in the eye, muscle cramps, ulcers; gives courage and endurance; calms, relaxes, and reduces emotional upsets.

LAPIS: A mental and spiritual cleanser; brings wisdom; good for blood, fever, melancholia, neuralgia, tonsils and throat, bronchial passages, menstruation; stimulates mental clarity and discipline; invigorates thymus.

MALACHITE: Brings prosperity, treats the eyes and abnormal blood sugar levels; treats circulatory diseases, awakens and regenerates healers, clears stuck emotions, promotes sleep, corrects right/left brain disorders and mental illnesses; good for the heart; mirrors the soul.

MILKY QUARTZ: Gets us in touch with the hidden, invisible, mysterious, and elusive—within and without.

MOONSTONE: A calming stone, good for meditation; gives spiritual guidance and protection while traveling. A love stimulator, brings happy experiences to those who are sensitive; a psychic opener; used for prophecy, realizing hopes, and emotional release; best used in jewelry or on wands; teaches you to flow with things, enhances wisdom gained through experience; excellent for female problems of all kinds.

QUARTZ CRYSTAL (CLEAR/WHITE): Raises one's vibrations, bridges the material world with higher realms; holds, stores, amplifies, and transmits energy; excellent for all types of healing work and meditation practices; gives increased sensitivity to subtle energies, attunement to Mother Earth and the preservation of her resources; for attunement to Sacred Sites and the planetary crystal grid system; for the universal mind and God-consciousness, contact with other dimensions and spiritual and cosmic beings; speeds up your evolutionary process, promotes clarity and wisdom; facilitates memory, transformation, awakening, cleansing; enhances positive thoughts and prayers; brings emotional, physical, mental and spiritual balance.

ROSE QUARTZ: Brings more love into the life; promotes skin rejuvenation; in promoting the filtering process of the kidneys, opens the heart *chakra* for receiving and sharing love; helps cure loneliness; heals grief, depression, sense of loss, abused children; brings joy and happiness.

SMOKY QUARTZ: Helps one get more in touch with nature; excellent for meditation and healing on the mental and etheric levels; carries an ultra-sound frequency which enables one to develop clairaudience and mediumship.

TIGER EYE: Purifies the system after over-indulgence; treats diseases of the eye; a protective stone.

TOURMALINE: A very powerful healing tool which vibrates all the *chakras* at one time. Green tourmaline relieves chronic fatigue, attracts prosperity; pink sends your love out into the world and says it is safe to love, releasing old destructive feelings; black deflects negative energy, neutralizes one's own negativity, helps one stay spiritual when surrounded by unconscious people; watermelon color is for those who do counseling work and for healing relationships; it balances emotions and the metabolism.

TURQUOISE: Reminding us of our spiritual nature, it has to do with the atmosphere surrounding the Earth; gives protection; is good for the heart, chest, neck, lung, respiratory system, and eyes; a Master Healer; a stone of peace, tranquillity, prosperity, and good luck, used for remembrance of past lives and promoting long-term friendship.

CLEANING THE CRYSTAL

Since crystals interact with the positive and negative energies around them, you will want to clean your new crystals. Ultra-violet light can cleanse them of negative energies, so placing them out in the sun for a couple of hours is recommended. For light cleansing, use mild soap and warm water. For deep cleansing, use sea salt and distilled water. Dry them in the sun. They can be *energized* by sunlight or moonlight at any time.

THE USE OF CRYSTALS IN MEDITATION AND HEALING

When meditating, hold your crystal in your left hand, or place it on your body. If it is pointed, let the point face you.

Because of their electromagnetic properties, crystals can aid in healing by encouraging the proper energy flow throughout the body. Hold the crystal in your left hand, on the area to be healed, for thirty minutes, giving a prayer of thanks before and after each healing session.

In all cases, relax and clear your mind, first, so that you may concentrate on the question or concern at hand. Let the crystal's energy flow to the specific area you wish to treat, and *see* that area, in your mind's eye, in a new and healed state.

DEVELOPING YOUR PSYCHIC POTENTIAL

Now that you have seen how people can perceive higher, psychic vibrations, let's get down to the business of learning a few methods of psychic unfoldment. These methods include how to see and read an aura; send and receive telepathic impressions; meditate; heal; interpret dreams; discern intuitively; and keep an ESP journal.

Psychic and *spiritual* powers are different things entirely. Psychic unfoldment is the awakening of a psychic awareness within— beyond the five physical senses. Spiritual unfoldment is the awakening of the soul to the realities of existence: in other words, practicing faith and service toward one's fellow man.

Supernormal refers to psychic powers because they vary from the normal in a constructive manner. *Supernatural* refers to an exception to natural law. In ordinary science, supernatural refers to things that cannot be explained in scientific terms. In psychic science, there are no supernatural events: All psychic phenomena are natural and normal and, therefore, not "above" natural law, not "super" natural.

I have often heard people say, in regard to psychic phenomena, "I'll believe it when I see it." Actually, in light of modern scientific knowledge, this is a ridiculous statement. The human eye is blind to about 98 percent of the light waves known to science. Whatever we "look" like to another human eye is strictly a matter of the physical light in which we are seen. For example, if a performer wearing white has a blue spotlight shining on him, he looks blue to us. Are you fooled into thinking he really has a strange skin disorder which makes him appear blue? How about the way we look under an X-ray machine? Of course, you may argue that previous knowledge and experience teach us that the performer under the blue lights is only reflecting the color blue, and that really his skin is white or black. Well, what I'm asking you to do is learn that things are not necessarily what our *five* senses tell us they are. As science continues to prove, reality is subjective.

Once you learn and experience a more open way of looking at the world, these perceptions and concepts—which might seem strange to you now—will seem quite natural.

Before you embark on your study of psychic enrichment, remember this: Be patient, and don't try to grasp everything at once. All is revealed to those who work hard and earnestly at something worthwhile, and your study of psychic and spiritual sciences is certainly in that category.

KEEPING AN ESP JOURNAL

Keeping an ESP journal will help you document your progress. This daily written record of psychic experiences includes meditations as well as spontaneous occurrences. According to the psychic laws of symbolism and imagery, you may receive psychic messages in your dreams. After a while, you will learn the many things from your subconscious mind to which you formerly paid little attention.

A good journal, maintained faithfully, should contain the following:

1. All supernatural and psychic experiences
2. Dates for each entry
3. The place and conditions at the time of the experience
4. Space on each page to note whether the experience or message received was verified.

A sample entry might look like this:

June 5, 1985

2:15 P.M.—Sitting at my desk and overcome with horrible feeling. Felt extremely uneasy. Doesn't seem to be a result of anything from work.

(Later learned [sister] Sally had an appendicitis attack at 2:00 and was rushed to the hospital.)

COINCIDENCE, INTUITION, AND DISCERNMENT

Some people wonder if occasional psychic-type experiences are just coincidence, not true psychic occurrences. Over and over again, you hear people say they have a "hunch," a "gut feeling," or a "woman's intuition." Others say, "Something told me . . ." Those who act on these hunches almost always find that their inner feelings were correct. All these experiences are examples of the extrasensory perception of which we all are capable and which we need only to develop.

There is, in fact, no simple way to distinguish between intuition and wishful thinking. It takes much faith, patience, and practice to develop one's intuition. When a person first begins to develop psychic abilities, it is a self-realization process. You must get to know yourself and your abilities well enough to tell the difference. At first, it's a trial-and-error proposition. Eventually, you will "just know" whether the information you receive is psychic or not. Ultimately, discernment becomes easy. Take your time, be honest with yourself, and trust that you will develop these capabilities. There should be no shame or sense of failure if they do not come right away. You may have lived a long time without exercising your mind in this way, and, as with atrophied muscles, strengthening and practice are necessary for success.

I sometimes encounter people who question the origin of the information I receive. Many of these people are not as interested in understanding the difference between wishful thinking and intuition as they are in whether my intuition is coming from good or evil sources. From a biblical standpoint, this understanding is called "discernment."

One could question the "divine" information received by today's religious leaders like Oral Roberts or Billy Graham. These leaders say God talks to them. Yet, because they preach a more "mainstream" approach, their statements remain uncontested. In truth, there is no way to really know the origin of their transcendental information, except by looking at the person's present and past history, past actions, and past deeds. In my case, with the belief that God was all-powerful, prayer was always a part of my life. I have always considered myself a positive, spiritual person, rational, balanced, and with no history of emotional or mental instability. I never initially *invited* psychic/spiritual experiences to happen, because I had no exposure to anything of that nature. Psychic/spiritual experiences just started happening to me on their own.

The psychic/spiritual information I received was always positive and guided me in the right direction, continually influencing me to stay on the right path. In 1969, after attending the Fort Lauderdale Church of the Master Jesus in which Jewell Williams was the minister, I developed—through meditation and religious study—a greater understanding of what I was experiencing. It was after this time that I developed my clairaudient abilities, as recounted earlier in this book. This enabled me to actually hear the spiritual voices.

Since these spiritual revelations and experiences made me feel good and happy and were so uplifting, I felt this was a gift from God meant to allow me to help others. The thought that they might be of Satanic origin, as some fundamentalists believe, never entered my mind.

The information received through "hearing" was the same as that I received through impressions. As with many other people, *impressions* are the way in which I usually receive information. To this day, I have never had a feeling or heard a voice telling me to do anything bad or strange. I have never had a negative experience result from what I was told psychically/spiritually/intuitively. This is proof enough, for me, that my abilities are good and God-given.

VOICES

I don't feel that, because I hear a voice speak to me, I am unusual. Many philosophers, novelists, saints, poets, military leaders, athletes, and scientists have heard voices. Going back in history, Saint Teresa, Socrates, Carl Jung, and Joan of Arc all claimed to hear spiritual voices. And, more recently—according to a 1985 Gallup poll—some sixteen million Americans have heard voices.

People often are reluctant to share these experiences, for fear of what others may think. Considering that hearing voices is one sign of mental illness, these fears as well founded. But the voices of mental illness are intrusive, condemning, abusive and/or tyrannical. Psychiatrists call this phenomenon "auditory hallucinations," a widely recognized sign of schizophrenia. This particular form of mental illness affects about one percent of our population.

According to Fort Lauderdale psychiatrist Dr. Richard Maulion, hearing voices is but one symptom, which in itself does not make a diagnosis of psychosis. Other symptoms are needed, which may include thought disorders, the presence of delusions, and/or a departure from reality. The severity of the psychosis can be from mild to severe, with all the varying degrees in between. Frequently, this departure from reality is accompanied by hearing voices, and often these voices are negative: They put the person down, tell him he is no good, may even tell him to walk on glass or jump out the window. When there is no thought disorder or impairment of reality, and a "normal" individual hears voices, the diagnosis deals in a "gray," uncertain area. For this reason, psychiatry needs to be respectful of its own ignorance, as there remains much we do not know or understand. An open mind on the subject is essential.

The fact is, voices *are* heard by perfectly sane, rational people, and the voices they hear provide spiritual guidance. They do not *interfere* with a person's life; rather, they add a richer spiritual dimension, a higher consciousness, a greater awareness. The Bible, and religious writings of all faiths, are filled with accounts of the devout hearing voices.

Psychologist Mary Watkins, author of *Invisible Guests*, says that, "where a voice comes from is not as important as what it is saying. When you listen to it, you can learn things you are not often receptive to." Alfred Alschuler, a clinical psychologist and Professor of Education at the University of Massachusetts at Amherst, is among those who hear voices. The voice he hears is not his own, he says, but he can tune into it whenever he likes. "At first, it was like going to a lecture," he explains. "I just listened and wrote down whatever I heard." He has heard information on a number of spiritual topics, from love to the afterlife, and says that—as a result of these experiences—he has become less materialistic and more patient and loving. Although he cannot be certain where this voice comes from, he says he knows it deals with "high ideals and the relationship to God."

THE HUMAN AURA

Think of the phrases, "green with envy" and "so angry I was seeing red." It is no coincidence that we use colors to describe our moods. My ability to see the human aura (energy vibrations surrounding people) has made me realize there is an unconscious psychic basis for these and other, similar sayings.

Extensive studies have been done on the effect of colors on our lives, and we have learned that wearing certain colors reflects our moods or personalities. The colors we choose to decorate our homes and offices can affect our state of mind, just as specific colors have long been chosen for the walls of hospitals and schools. Visible colors are interpreted by our eyes according to their specific wave lengths; each one has its own vibration.

A study done by the University of Northern Colorado suggests that red has the power to arouse us and make us more aggressive. The theory indicates that wearing red or decorating your office with red accents helps you to become more confident and dynamic. Yellow stirs the creative juices; blue has a calming effect; green promotes rationality; purple reflects spiritual qualities. Police have tried painting the walls of holding cells blue, in hopes of calming potentially violent prisoners, and other experiments have suggested that painting hospital walls pink or light orange stimulates healing. We should be aware of the possible individual effect colors have on us and use them wisely.

Violet, traditionally considered a highly spiritual and intuitive color, is recommended for meditation, because it relaxes and soothes the nerves and the muscles controlling the heart. Leonardo da Vinci said that meditation's power increased tenfold when done under rays of violet falling through the stained-glass windows of a quiet church.

Colors can have physical effects on other living things, as well. Dr. Camille Flammarion, a French psychic researcher, found that lettuce placed under a red glass grows four times as fast as usual when in direct sunlight. Under green glass, oxidation was increased, and under blue the plant's growth was stunted.

Even more important than those colors easily discernible to the human eye are the colors in a person's aura. We sometimes refer to the aura as "the human atmosphere." It is an electromagnetic energy field consisting of vibrations and radiations of energies which come from the outer surface of the body and flow in all directions. In their book *Magnetism and Its Effects on the Living System*, Albert Roy Davis and Walter C. Rawls, Jr., say, "We have surfaces on the body that are in a sense a radiation of electromagnetic energies. This statement is made in this broad manner as these energies are composed of many different forms, frequencies, microvoltages, and currents. This does not change the fact that they are present, projected from the surface of the body at all points."

With a little practice, you can see other people's auras, and you will find this ability invaluable in ascertaining their state of mind, intentions, and general health. The aura has been perceived through the ages by many saints and sages. It is known in their writings as the "halo," the "aureola," or the "glory." Religious paintings frequently show a halo of light around the Madonna and child, or around the head of Buddha, or surrounding Moses (making him "impossible to look upon"), and in the transfiguration of Jesus, when his robe shown so brightly that "no fuller on earth could whiten it." All these are descriptions of the aura.

Once again, modern science has proven what the mystics have known for ages. Dr. Walter J. Kilner, of St. Thomas Hospital in London, wrote the first scientific book on auras just after World War I. It was he who called the aura "the human atmosphere" and used mechanical means to see it—devising an "aura screen" by cementing sheets of glass together into a box shape and filling the tank with a solution of coal-tar dye. He claimed that, after looking through this screen for a few moments, he could look at a subject and perceive the aura with the naked eye.

Kilner divided auras into three distinct parts. First was the *etheric double*, a narrow black band closely hugging a person's outline. Immediately surrounding the etheric double was the *inner aura*, a semiluminous band extending about five inches from the body. Finally, extending several inches more from the inner aura was the *outer aura*, an oval shape surrounding the individual. Dr. Kilner believed the aura varied in size, form, and brightness according to the person's sex, age, and health.

Another part of the aura, in addition to those found by Dr. Kilner, can be seen and used for interpretations of emotional and physical well-being. This is a pulsating rainbow of colors, which can be "seen" around the head and shoulders. The colors coincide directly with both physical health and psychological and emotional makeup. ("Seeing" refers to sight with the psychic or "third" eye, not the physical eye.)

All things have a permanent aura. Even an inanimate object such as a rock has a stable, permanent aura. Living beings have both a permanent and a temporary aura. The permanent aura reveals the basic qualities or characteristics, while the temporary aura changes colors according to moods, emotions, physical health, and other surrounding influences.

KIRLIAN PHOTOGRAPHY

Scientific studies have proven that auras exist. Now, photographs can be taken of auras, using specially designed, highly sensitive equipment and a technique called "Kirlian photography," after the Russian couple who perfected it in 1939. (The Russians have a long history of investigating all areas of psychic phenomena. The book

Psychic Discoveries Behind the Iron Curtain, which caused such a sensation in the United States in the 1950s and 1960s, revealed for the first time the extent and seriousness of this research.)

Kirlian photography is also known as *radiation field photography, color electron emission photography*, and *electrophotography*. For many years, scientists had been aware that an energy field surrounded all living things, but the Kirlians developed a new kind of photography that uses no optical system, no light, and no bellows. It actually takes pictures of the radiation fields around living objects. Semyon and Valentina Kirlian examined objects and found the vibrational field around each to be significantly different. But the greatest difference was between living and nonliving things.

The Kirlians found that varying species of plants had different patterns of radiation emanating from them and, more important, that diseased leaves, compared to healthy leaves from the same plant, had distinctly different patterns. The disease showed up in the aura long before the plant showed any outward signs of ill health. They found this to be true in humans and animals, as well.

Eventually, the Kirlians were able to invent an optical device that reflected the subject's illness and mood changes, state of mind, fatigue, and other physical factors. Clairvoyants had been seeing auras for centuries, but no photographs had ever been taken of this phenomenon before the Kirlians developed their technique. It is now evident that clairvoyants may be able to see around and into the human body in a much more efficient, less harmful way than with the use of X rays.

In Kirlian photography today, a piece of sheet film is placed on an electrically charged flat piece of metal. The fingertips are placed directly on the film, and the plate is then charged with alternating current (AC) at low amperage. The aura around the fingertip is thought to expose the film. The result is an aura that looks like a series of lines of energy forming a pattern. This pattern shows the energy given off and the subject's state of being.

If the emanations are strong and straight, it is an indication of good general health. If auric radiations look ragged or weak, general health is poor. Bright, clear lines also are an indication of good health, as opposed to dark, varying, or wobbly lines, which indicate ill health. The strength and shape of the lines also indicate the person's emotional state.

Unfortunately, there is no standardized Kirlian equipment, today, with the result that—since every aura picture is different—analysis can be difficult and open to broad interpretation. This is an area in which computer analysis might provide better answers.

The possible practical applications for Kirlian photography are many, in both human and plant-related fields. Since the emotional interactions between people can be measured in this way, there are possibilities for use in psychoanalysis, while agricultural interests could use it to test crops for developing disease. In medicine and dentistry and in any field where diagnostics are an important part of the healing or fixing process, the possibilities are far-reaching.

Another area in which Kirlian photography has found a place is treatment by acupuncture. Acupuncture meridians travel down the fingers and toes, ending at the tips—corresponding with the areas spotlighted in Kirlian photographs. This link may prove to be one of the most productive lines of research in scientific aura diagnosis and analysis.

AURA DIAGNOSIS

Following are the generally accepted aura color interpretations:

BLACK: catastrophe, disaster, extreme depression and/or unhappiness; physical death or death of a circumstance; intense negativity, disease.

GRAY: depression, unhappiness, poor health, passive
negativity, fear, and dissatisfaction.

RED: anxiety, tension, vigor, energy, forcefulness, undue
stress, lack of communication, passion, frustration.

BROWN: passion, aggression, and intense emotions.

BLUE: spiritual acceptance varying with the shade of
blue manifested, loyalty, prayerful nature, contempla-
tive, positive, dedicated.

GREEN: healing, financial gains, service to others, peaceful, changeful, creative, helpful.

PINK: affection, love, maternal, sensitive, caring, compassion.

YELLOW: optimistic, intelligent, successful, positive, favorable, honest, cheerful, sign of growth, productive.

PURPLE: spiritual, protective, leadership, positive, powerful, transmuting.

WHITE: spiritual, enlightened, pure, integrity, trustwor-
thy, harmony, cosmic attunement, positive attitude,
successful divine love (the highest color to attain and
maintain).

There are various shades of intensity in each color seen in the
aura, indicating different shades of emotional, spiritual, or physical
health. A dull or dark tone of the color is more negative than a
bright tone.

Learning to see people's auras has plenty of obvious benefits. If
you could look at someone and be able to make a quick, sure judgment about whether he or she has hidden anger or limited intellectual ability, wouldn't it be helpful in screening that person for a
job, or even for a personal relationship? People can lie with words,
but they cannot hide evidence of emotional and physical distress in
the aura. Of course it must be remembered that a person's aura

changes moment by moment, as his emotions cool or heat up and actual *thoughts* cannot be ascertained through the aura-reading technique.

As one who has been able to read auras for many years, now, I have found it most helpful in screening out people who will not be compatible or helpful to me in my life and mission. I also use this ability to understand a person's physical problems, by interpreting his aura's colors.

We have now learned ways to see the aura which are better and easier than Dr. Kilner's "screen." One is to place a very low wattage lamp on the floor behind the individual, allowing you to study him without straining. Another is to gaze at yourself in the mirror, attempt to see the three parts of the aura, and then *sense* the colors. One technique I think works especially well is the following:

1. Be comfortable and mentally at ease.
2. Choose a subject.
3. Have the person sit in front of a light-colored background.
4. Observe, without staring at your subject. Fix your gaze and be aware of the energy field surrounding the person.
5. Do not expect to see just one solid color, but many colors with varying intensities and hues. Equate seeing with feeling.

What your mind perceives, your eye sees. Therefore, if your mind tells you the color is red or green, translate that into its proper interpretation. The interpretation of what you are feeling or seeing will come to you intuitively and spiritually from that God-force within you. Remember, you are an open channel through which this Intelligence functions, if you allow it. The information you wish to obtain usually is related to the subject's complex state of being. This complexity can be broken down into categories, including business, finance, family health, psychic and spiritual development, negative influences surrounding the person, relationships, travel, and personal concerns.

For example, if I feel or see red around a person, I most often receive an impression of the particular category to which this color relates. The speed of interpretation comes with practice. In the beginning, you may find it will help you to run through the above-listed categories mentally and correlate the color to the specific area and its appropriate interpretation.

With experience, you will be able to differentiate the permanent color or colors from the temporary colors brought about by changing physical, emotional, or spiritual circumstances. You should not limit yourself to practicing in a controlled setting. Do it at any time, any place. Try it in a shopping mall, a park, or even when walking down the street. Just be aware that everyone has an aura. Try to "feel" it with your mind, then try to actually see it.

To test the accuracy of the impressions perceived, it will help to keep a log of your attempts, entering the person's name and the state of his or her well-being as of that date. Jot down your impressions and, whenever possible, question the subject to verify the accuracy of your impressions. If a friend comes to visit, sits down, and has a cup of coffee, observe and interpret his aura (silently, to yourself), then verify what you have seen and felt about his state of mind and the circumstances in the various areas of his life.

Don't expect to be 100 percent accurate. Even the most highly acclaimed psychics are not that accurate. As with everything in life, it takes practice and discipline to develop any of the psychic and spiritual abilities, but the rewards are great. It is not necessary to be spiritual to have psychic abilities; everyone has hunches and feelings that can be developed into real abilities when practiced. However, spiritual people normally do exhibit a greater natural intuitive ability in the paranormal area, as they tend to be more sensitive and tend to communicate more easily with the Higher Intelligence (God) through prayer, inspiration, voice contact, visions, and the like, than the person who is interested only in the psychic aspect. The development of the spiritual and psychic part of your holistic being will help you to help others, as in seeing their auras you become more aware of everyone's emotional, spiritual, and physical characteristics and needs.

TELEPATHY AND IMPRESSIONALISM

The most prevalent way to pick up thoughts and feelings is through telepathy. Because it is the most common form of ESP, it is the easiest for people to understand and accept. Telepathic thought transference is recognized in all forms of psychic and parapsychological research. It is defined as "the transference of mental states from one individual directly to another individual without physical agency."

We have already established that "thoughts are things," which—once created—have a life of their own and can have a concrete effect on people and on the physical world. Now consider the responsibility which comes when one learns to actually intercept the thoughts of others and to transmit thoughts into someone else's conscious or subconscious mind. Properly used, it becomes a new form of communication, with very exciting possibilities.

There are many kinds of telepathy, but generally they are grouped in three broad classifications:

1. *Individual telepathy*—takes place within one person as a communication between the higher self and the brain.
2. *Mutual telepathy*—takes place between two individuals.

3. *Group telepathy*—takes place between groups or between an individual and a group.

Individual telepathy is perhaps the most important of the
three. It involves establishing channels of communication between
you and your subconscious mind. This is accomplished through
meditation, which I shall describe at length later in this section.

Mutual telepathy can be of four types: emotional, mental, or
soul telepathy, or any combination of two or three simultaneously.

Most likely, everyone has experienced *emotional telepathy*—
actually feeling what another person, who is close to you, feels. The
phenomenon rarely occurs over great distances. This form of telepathy does not involve verbal thoughts, only feelings of love, hate,
fear, etc.

Mental telepathy is a technique that usually requires a great deal
of practice, but it is one which has proven to be extremely reliable.
It is difficult to cultivate the power to read another's *thoughts*, but we
find that *images* are far more easily transmitted. You have probably
had many telepathic experiences of this sort that you simply didn't
recognize. You may have been concentrating on someone late at
night who phoned the next morning, saying he was thinking of you
and just had to call. Or you could be sitting with a friend and have
the feeling she is going overseas, only to find out, a few minutes later,
that she's planning a trip to Europe.

A reputable teacher or class on the subject will help you become more adept at telepathy. In the meantime, you may find the
following steps will begin to prepare you:

1. The channel between sender and receiver must be
   kept completely open. Any negative thoughts or
   emotions such as impatience, suspicion, or resentment will impair reception.

2. The sender must concentrate extremely hard on her message. The mind has a tendency to wander. Even to think too much about the receiver will cause a break in contact.

3. The receiver should think of the sender for just a short time; then, after sending a strong feeling of love, put her and her personality completely out of mind. He must be relaxed and open but remain completely indifferent.

4. The receiver should achieve a state of complete mental quietude, a cutting off of the "internal dialogue" that is always at work in our mind. Such thoughts will block out any incoming thought energy.

Soul telepathy is a very advanced form of telepathy which involves the communication of the superconscious or higher self between individuals or with God.

The most common way to receive psychic or spiritual information is through impressions that are communicated telepathically. A psychic impression is a hunch, thought, idea, or feeling that explains or interprets a vision you see or a vibration you feel. It may come independently of other forms of psychic communication. Psychic impressions often are received through a telepathic process directed from a spiritual being or your guardian angel. At other times, your impressions result from your attunement with your higher self (individual telepathy). It takes time, prayer, meditation, metaphysical study, and adherence to holistic principles to make things even clearer, so that you receive more accurate, detailed information.

Learning to discern and differentiate between a psychic impression and a normal, everyday impression is important. Do not confuse a desire with an impression. Just because a cup of coffee and a doughnut pop into your mind at 9 A.M. doesn't mean your guardian angel is impressing you to drink coffee and eat a doughnut. That's what your body desires; it is not a spiritual suggestion. Be realistic. Use your common sense. Through the meditation techniques in the next section, you will learn more about recognizing impressions and other psychic experiences.

MEDITATION

As mentioned earlier, *alpha* brain waves, which are much slower than our waking brain waves, come into play during meditation. Meditation cannot be overemphasized as a method of bringing our latent psychic potential to the surface. In fact, meditation is really the cornerstone of getting in touch with the higher vibrations. There is now scientific evidence that meditation can prolong life. Harvard University researchers have reported a lowering of blood pressure and an improvement in mental function in elderly people who, after learning Transcendental Meditation, lived longer than their peers.

Meditation is "listening"—listening to that quiet, all-knowing voice within each of us. You could also call it listening to God. Prayer—speaking to God—is the reciprocal of meditation. With meditation done in the proper spirit (a positive, receptive frame of mind) and with adequate preparation, you will open yourself to the spiritual forces that exist in the ethereal world.

No specific aids such as mantras, candles, incense, or music are needed to meditate, although some people feel more comfortable using these aids. *No type of drug, hallucinogenic or otherwise, should be used while meditating.* Anything that unnaturally alters one's awareness has a detrimental, self-destructive effect on the total being and interferes with the process of spiritual illumination, which is the desired result of meditation. The use of drugs is also foreign to the holistic principles, as drugs cause physical damage to the body's cells and weaken the immune system. The best body instrument to receive higher communications is the one that is the strongest and purest it can be. You cannot separate body and mind, in keeping with holistic health.

An examination of self-motivation is necessary prior to meditation. *Sincerity, perseverance,* and *faith* must be present as a spiritual foundation before attempting to reach higher consciousness:

SINCERITY

Ask yourself, "Do I really want to know this Infinite Intelligence (God) and my connection to it? Am I willing to channel the information received to the benefit of others? Am I sincere in accepting myself and the role I play in the interconnectedness of love that flows through the universe?"

PERSEVERANCE

Mental and physical perseverance is another most important key to meditation. You must command your mind and body to be still. It is imperative to banish irrelevant thoughts and to concentrate on this Creative Intelligence. This is not an easy task. Only perseverance and daily observance, preferably in the same physical environment each day, will prove to God that you are serious in this undertaking.

FAITH

Faith is the third key factor in successful meditation. You must believe in this ultimate breakthrough in communication with the Higher Intelligence. Bring to this process an inner enthusiasm, remembering the deep faith displayed by the great spiritual masters and prophets such as Moses, Jesus, Mohammed, Buddha, and other disciples of faith. Concentrate on this faith, and don't be discouraged if you don't obtain immediate results. It may take weeks, months, or even years to attain an open channel of direct communication between you and God.

Determination, patience, and daily practice will bring results and will make your meditation period the single most important event in your daily routine. The most conducive times to meditate are upon rising and before retiring at night.

PHYSICAL PREPARATION FOR MEDITATION

1. The position in which you meditate is not important, but do not choose a position conducive to falling asleep. You may choose to sit upright in a straight-back chair with your head resting against the back, or you may decide to lie down. If you're comfortable in the classic cross-legged or "lotus" position, it, also, works very well. In any case, the spine should be straight, for proper breathing. You must be in a position that allows you to concentrate for an indeterminate amount of time without drawing your attention to various parts of your body.

2. Deep breathing is another vital tool, because it charges the body with electromagnetic energy, called in yogic schools *prana*, the life force. This pranic energy stimulates the psychic and spiritual centers housed in the physical body. Slowly take five to ten deep breaths, in and out, to the count of ten. You will see how this practice calms, revitalizes, and attunes your being to God. (This is an excellent way to relax and "center" yourself, at any time of stress or confusion.)

3. To facilitate concentration, it is important that the body be in balance. This applies, first of all, to the diet. The interplay of the holistic concept (body, mind, and soul) becomes evident even in our preparation for meditation. Gastric distress from eating improper

foods will cause a physical body imbalance that will interfere with the meditation process. The study of nutrition is extremely valuable in assuring you get the most out of meditation.

MENTAL PREPARATION FOR MEDITATION

1. Clear your mind of all extraneous thoughts. Each time a thought, whether pleasant or disturbing, enters your conscious mind, it is a distraction. Remove the intruding thought by "willing" it out: Visualize a closed door. Outside thoughts may knock on the door, but you refuse to answer. You remain content and peaceful inside, as you have learned to block out all intrusions. This technique will help you in all areas of your life, especially during those times when you are faced with unpleasant circumstances. Clearing or blanking the mind is not the easiest task for those who have never before controlled their thought processes (or were aware they could). However, with constant practice, everyone can master this capability.

2. If you are harboring any ill will against anyone for whatever reason, justified or not, you must release this negativity to the Universal Intelligence. This negativity will only block the mental passivity required for spiritual attunement. Use the Law of Transmutation and get rid of it. Remember, the scales always have to balance (karma) and everyone does get his just reward.

3. Use affirmations such as: "I am now open to mental passivity; I am relaxed, calm and peaceful"; "Nothing can interfere with my inner serenity"; or "I am emotionally and mentally poised." You can make up your own. Whatever feels good to you and works is all that counts.

4. Program for results. Impress your subconscious mind with goal-oriented requests. For example, "I will achieve the following goals in the immediate future: (1) Be able to maintain a calm mind

under all circumstances, especially during meditation; (2) Achieve definite psychic abilities in the areas of healing and clairvoyance; (3) With my inner and outer serenity, I will be of great service to people."

SPIRITUAL PREPARATION FOR MEDITATION

1. Spiritually open your meditation session with a protective affirmation such as: "May the great white light of God surround me and bring only those things that are good and right to me." Repeat this as often as necessary, until you actually feel yourself surrounded by this white light and you feel peaceful, serene, and tranquil.

2. Choose a prayer or a spiritual reading you particularly like. Think about the meaning of the prayer or reading, rather than repeat it word for word. Whatever prayer you use is fine; it is the sincerity that matters. Here is a spiritual preparedness reading you may choose to use:

> Dear God:
> I come to You this day with deep love and devotion in my heart, to do Your Will and to become ever closer to You through the disciplining of my lower self and obeying Your universal laws. I ask that my angels and all Your spiritual representatives be with me at this time, to help me. I am receptive to their energies. Forgive me my transgressions and also those who have transgressed against me. Use me as a channel for Your everlasting love and light. Open my body, mind, and soul to Your wisdom, so that I may better understand You and know Your Will for me. Because I know I am to praise and thank You for all things, no matter how big or small, I am now praising and thanking You for all my circumstances, difficulties,

problems, and irritations. These, I know, are necessary for my spiritual growth. I learn from them. As I praise You, I see my worries, troubles, and sorrows all surrounded by Your brilliant white light of love, protection, and healing.

Continue to lead and guide me to do and say the right things, to choose the right friends, eat and drink the right food and water, read constructive books, breathe clean air, think only positive thoughts.

I will learn to meditate before I act. I realize that meditation followed by action is the key to a balanced existence of spiritual communion and active service to my fellow man.

Amen

Among the affirmations you may wish to use are the following:

I am now open to healing.
I am now open to love.
I am now open to prosperity.
I am now open to spiritual bliss.
I am now open only to positive thoughts.
I now know health, vitality, energy, and strength.
I now attract only good into my life.

3. Think of yourself as a channel of clear intuition acquired through meditation. You are filled with love and understanding as a result of applying the universal laws, a knowledge that will help not only you but also those who come in contact with you, making you an integral link in the chain of universal creation.

4. Ask God, the all-knowing Intelligence, to reveal the truth to you about any situation or individual that concerns you. Ask to be

shown various signs indicating your path in the right direction. These cosmic signs can come from literally any person, place, thing, or feeling. If you find yourself becoming increasingly unhappy or disturbed in a particular situation or relationship, you may be assured the universe is telling you that you need to reevaluate the circumstance. Maybe it is time to stop pursuing that particular endeavor; perhaps changing jobs or ending a relationship is in order. Answers from the higher source may pop up coincidentally. You may pick up a psychology magazine while waiting in the dentist's office and find the solution there. Then again, listening to a friend's advice might help. Prepare yourself emotionally to accept the truth and deal with it. Should the truth be disturbing or unpleasant, sincerely praise God for it. It is through the law of praise that you reaffirm your loyalty and faith. Through these experiences, you are making yourself more worthy to be the channel for God's everlasting spiritual enlightenment. The rewards you gain by praising and accepting this enlightenment will prove to you there are cosmic reasons for every circumstance, and that something better always comes if you expect it.

5. Realize you are opening yourself to communication with God and His angels and spirit representatives. As He promised us, He will send legions of angels to help us, so we should make use of this powerful assistance by calling upon these angelic beings. You may also see or feel the presence of angels or spiritual teachers who work with us in our endeavors to evolve spiritually. You may see or feel the presence of familiar beings who have gone beyond into the next dimension (family members or other loved ones).

6. This state of readiness should never be confused with a state of trance because at all times you will be consciously aware of your surroundings. Do not be frightened by any spiritual contact made through meditation. Know that your attunement to God repels any negative vibrations and thus brings only what is in your best interest. This God-force is a vibrating sea of energy, of pulsating,

brilliant white light. God is manifested in the "white light" so often described in spiritual books. Visualize, receive, and accept this energy as a protective force permeating your being and surrounding you like a protective shield, on all sides, at all times.

PASSIVE PHASE OF MEDITATION

You have just completed the *active* phase of your preparation for meditation. What follows now is the *passive* phase—for most of us, the more difficult part. It is during this period, having put everything in order, that you are now passively awaiting the actual psychic and spiritual communication breakthrough. Do not be discouraged if, after following all the aforementioned preparations to the letter, you do not gain instant illumination. You must prove yourself persistently, by an honest and sincere effort of perseverance and faith, to be worthy of this divine guidance. As I have said before, this combination is necessary not only initially but continually, to demonstrate to this Divine Intelligence that we have the inspired determination to communicate.

Intelligent awareness of what to expect during this passive waiting period becomes a major part in your meditation process. Compare yourself to a switchboard. You will attract many calls, but—like an inexperienced operator—you might not be able to make the connections quickly. In the beginning, you may find that you make a psychic/spiritual connection of sorts, but through inexperience you may lose or wrongly interpret it. If you receive a spiritual message, vision, or impression, hear a voice, or see an aura, make note of it in a detached manner, keeping your cosmic lines open. If a spiritual/psychic connection is broken, don't try to force reattunement. Remain passive, and God or your angelic assistants will present it to you again. Be patient.

For some begining students of meditation, it will be possible to achieve an awareness of the God-force within, sometimes called the *higher self*, without drawing upon the energies of various spiritual beings. This higher consciousness within ourselves is always present to give us guidance and answers, just as its spiritual representatives are ever ready to help us in the attainment of our holistic goals.

I usually suggest that beginning students of metaphysics meditate from fifteen to thirty minutes, twice a day—preferably in the early morning and again before retiring.

Reassure yourself that psychism is not a special gift possessed by a select few but, rather, is part of your heritage as a child of the universe.

MEDITATION SYMBOLS

Meditation has a language all its own. Let's talk, first, about personal symbols.

If you receive a symbol during meditation and don't get an immediate interpretation, ask the Divine Intelligence (mentally) for the meaning. It will come to you as an impression or feeling. Make note of it and store it in your conscious mind. More than likely you will—in the future—recognize this symbol and its interpretation. In time you will develop your own personal repertoire of symbolic language.

While you will most likely be given an immediate psychic insight into the meaning of these symbols, there are certain, universal symbols, such as a cross, a baby, and a butterfly, which have accepted, specific meanings. Knowing these will help you develop a fast and efficient form of communication with the Higher Intelligence during meditation. A few of these universal symbols are listed here, but keep in mind that all symbols are open to interpretation:

Statue of Liberty	freedom
Grim Reaper	death
· School	education
Food	nourishment
Bed	sleep
Water	purification
Open hand	friendship
Bird	messenger
Letter	news
Boat	travel

Thoughts or ideas always accompany the reception of a symbol or image, to help explain what it means. Don't expect 100 percent perfection when interpreting dreams or meditational impressions. Practice and experience will greatly increase your degree of proficiency.

As you end the passive phase of the meditation period, say a closing prayer of thanks and praise for God's assistance as the Infinite Intelligence, and for the assistance of His spiritual representatives.

Through the steps outlined in this meditation process, you are gaining knowledge and building a bridge between Eastern and Western philosophies. It has been said that the religions of the West, although full of action and energy, tend to spend little time acquiring that deep spiritual knowledge which is so necessary to live in harmony with man and the universe. Ideally, the result should be a blend of the two: in other words, meditation followed by action. This constitutes the holistic way.

BREATHING

Proper breathing during meditation and during all waking moments helps you tune in to psychic vibrations. The tremendous importance of breathing is emphasized even in the Bible, where we are told the Creator "breathed upon the waters" to create life. Every living thing breaths, including plants, animals, and man.

Humans breathe at the rate of about sixteen breaths per minute, normally taking in about thirty cubic inches of air each time. Breathing consists of inhalation, exhalation, and a pause. The whole process should take about four heartbeats to complete. Most of us, however, do not breathe properly. The diaphragm (a large muscle at the base of the lungs) should bring the whole rib cage upward on inhalation, then force out the spent air on exhalation.

The *rhythm* of our breathing is more important still. Eastern religions have made a science of proper breathing, claiming that breathing is directly associated with longevity and mental and spiritual health. We know that, when we become excited, our breath quickens, and that when we try to calm ourselves, the quickest method is to lower the rate of breathing. If we slow our breath to ten or twelve breaths per minute, we find it impossible to become excited at all. (Try doing this for ten minutes, and you'll find yourself calmer and more stable, with a clearer mind.) Controlled breathing has a healing effect on our overall holistic health. It can aid in the reduction of stress, insomnia, and a wide variety of stress-related diseases. To control our physical health, therefore, it makes sense to start with this most basic aspect of our lives.

HEALING

No matter how hard we try to achieve perfect health and vitality, eventually something will go wrong with our bodies; yet most things can be remedied if they are caught early enough. For years, scientists have been baffled by the ancient healing approach of the "laying on of hands." Physicists at New York University are now studying the practices of Chinese healers, and investigation has validated the efficacy of their work. It has been shown that healing results from the hand's specific electromagnetic charge when it combines with the electromagnetic charge of the area the hand touches. Different parts of the body emit either positive or negative charges. Some zones are neutral.

Now magnets are being used to heal. According to the Albert Roy Davis Research Lab in Green Grove Springs, Florida, extensive tests have shown that the north pole of a magnet retards bacterial growth, takes away pain, reduces stress, and relaxes muscle tension, while the south pole stimulates growth and promotes healing. The magnetic energy can also be used in the treatment of disease.

Let's take a moment to analyze the word *disease*. It is a two-syllable word: *dis-ease*. When we separate the syllables, we see it is a matter of being ill at ease. Disease, often, is the physical manifestation of a mental stress condition. So-called miracle healings, I feel, are the positive spiritual energies directed through the physical body, giving the command to heal. The key is to be able to visualize this healing process. In my experience with healing over the years, I have improved my healing ability by working with the God-force within. As a result, I have been able to improve my clients' minor ailments, including headaches, emotional disorders, and minor pain. These clients usually feel a sense of relief and comfort, afterward—as though a burden has been lifted from them. A healing may last for days, weeks, or years.

HOW TO HEAL

When you prepared for meditation, you took the first steps toward opening your spiritual healing channel. To tap into your healing ability, follow these next steps:

1. Relax the body, using soothing music to set the mood and taking eight or ten deep breaths.

2. Using the suggestions previously outlined in Mental Preparation for Meditation, clear your mind of all extraneous thoughts.

3. Concentrate on the God-force within—the healing energy force, emanating as a brilliant, blinding white light. Surround yourself with this light, visualizing and feeling it as a positive, electrifying energy.

4. Ask to have this energy flow through and permeate your whole being. During this process, you may experience various signs or sensations, visions, tingling in the extremities, or the feeling of heat or cold. You may experience tightness or pressure in the forehead or neck region. All these sensations are signs that your "electrical" circuits are being activated. You may experience all or none of these signs, or you may have a feeling of complete relaxation and peace.

5. As in your individual meditation, begin by praising God for your problems and your blessings. Reaffirm that you do not hold resentment toward anything or anyone, as resentment blocks the flow of the healing energy. Praise speeds up the flow.

6. To use this healing energy, visualize it as a mental beam and direct it to the area that needs healing.

7. During the entire healing process, remember to give praise and thanks periodically for the healing. Ask God and His spiritual representatives to continue with the healing process, even after you have completed it.

8. Terminate each healing with a prayer, giving thanks to God and His angels and spiritual representatives (your Guardian Angels) for their healing energies.

HEALING OF OTHERS

To direct healing energy toward others, begin by projecting total un-selfish love toward the individual being healed, and feel like a part of him. Continue this throughout the healing. It is not necessary to have physical contact with this individual. You can perform absent healing—sending healing energy to someone who is not physically present. Long-distance healing takes intense concentration, so it is easier and more effective if you have physical contact when sending healing energies. This physical contact helps to establish more of a mental and spiritual rapport.

Following are the steps for healing others:

1. Instruct the recipient to sit in a chair. Stand behind him. Tell him to be open to the healing.

2. Put your hands on his shoulders. Feel that you are blending in with his aura. Relax your body with eight or ten deep breaths, and instruct him to do the same.

3. Clear your mind of all extraneous thoughts.

4. Surround yourself and your subject with the brilliant, blinding white light. Ask to have this energy flow through and per-meate your subject.

5. Praise God for your subject's maladies and blessings. Even if you do not know exactly what they are, give thanks anyway. God knows and will direct it to the right place. Always keep in mind that praise increases the healing energy. Because of this, make sure you give praise and thanks throughout the entire healing.

6. Lift your hands from his shoulders and proceed to move your hands around his aura, a few inches from his body. Allow your God-force within, as well as your guardian angel, to direct your hands. This may feel uncomfortable or unusual if you are not re-laxed. Any tension will block the flow of energy, so if you find this happening, return to step one and start over. If you don't feel your

hands drawn to any particular area, then consciously move them around slowly to different areas. Eventually, you will start feeling the energy flow. If you feel the recipient has problems with his feet, for example, it is not necessary to bring your hands to his feet; just visualize and mentally direct the healing energy to go there.

7. Continue in this manner for about ten to fifteen minutes, or until the healing is complete. As your healing comes to a close, your hands will be naturally drawn back to your subject's shoulders.

8. Again, give a prayer of thanks to God, to His angels and spiritual representatives, and to your guardian angels. Ask God to continue with this healing process.

It is even possible to heal someone you do not know and who is not in your presence. This type of healing may be done on one's own or in a group. Many feel that the combined energy of group healing is "more than the sum of its parts." In any case, relax first, with the name—or even just initials—of the person you wish to help. Visualize every area of his or her body, beginning at the top of the head and working downward, both externally and internally. Obviously, the internal "examination" will take longer, but picture each organ, all the nerves, muscles, and blood vessels, and "correct" anything that does not seem right to you. If you know the specific area of the person's problems, focus on that, particularly, but be sure to send light and energy for a "general healing" as well. In acute cases, you may wish to do this exercise several times each day. At the end of each session, picture the individual in glowing and robust health, sending him love and God's blessings for a speedy recovery.

During the healing process you may experience the same sensations you feel in meditation. You may even feel a powerful burst of energy going through your body, causing tremors in your arms and hands. Even in the absence of any physical sensations, you will be transmitting healing energy. Your subject may feel an immediate relief or a lessening of pain, or simply a feeling of peace. After giving a healing, many healers feel an increased vitality, as well.

The healing does not have to be instantaneous to help. The energy is never lost; it is always used in some way. Instant healings are actually quite rare; the vast majority of healing is gradual. Nor is a healing necessarily of a physical nature: Sometimes the healing goes toward a person's emotional health—perhaps over the course of several days. Several factors affect a healing. Some people are more receptive to this energy, and each healer channels and emits a different amount of energy. There also may be a specific divine reason why a healing is not achieved.

An example of such divine reason is in my own case. After my dramatic spiritual unfoldment in 1971, I continued to have migraine headaches. Even though my spiritual communication line was more open and I was studying nutrition and surrounding myself with medical and nutritional people, I still had the migraine headaches. I knew God could heal them but felt that, for some reason, it was not being done. One time, during an excrutiatingly bad headache cycle, I was sitting on my balcony in the middle of the night, tears streaming down my face, from pain. Looking at the floor, I suddenly saw a blue and white flash of light, right where I was looking, and in an instant the migraine was gone. Then I heard a voice say to me, "Yes, I can heal your headaches. But they will not be healed from prayer alone. There is more that has to be done." And so my search for a cure continued, with His guidance.

I feel strongly that, if you follow a holistic lifestyle, your speed of recovery will be much greater. Continuing to eat junk food, smoke, and drink alcohol, while praying for healing, obviously will slow the healing process dramatically. Remember, the main cause of disease, both emotional and physical, is our continued, repeated abuse of our bodies. Compared to physical abuse, mental abuse takes an even greater toll. This disease is caused by a lack of psychic (life force) energy, and some of the greatest consumers of psychic energy are worry, fear, resentment, and hurry. Don't let these things consume your energy. Take control of your emotions and channel them into positive feelings. The art of psychic healing is based on a positive, healthful state of mind. You cannot heal yourself, or anyone else for that matter, if you are sick or have low energy. Another psychic energy booster is to surround yourself daily with the white light. This helps protect you from any negative energies directed at you by other people. Think of this white light, which is drawn from your body and the Creative Source of the universe, as a reflective shield or armor. It is also a loving energy that, when directed toward anyone or anything, has tremendous healing power. You can draw upon this light with your mind energy at any time.

DREAMS AND THEIR IMPORTANCE

Most all of us have wished we could make better use of that one-third of our life we spend sleeping. But it is a myth that sleeping is simply a restful state our bodies use to recharge themselves. During sleep, important spiritual work is being done, and we can learn a great deal about ourselves and our purpose in life by recognizing the importance of sleep and dreams in psychic development.

When we sleep, we enter what is known as the *astral plane* or *astral world*, where reality is completely different from what we know in our waking hours. Astral matter is not defined by space or physical limitations, and we can shape and mold it with our minds. In this way, we can actually create situations or have conversations with people we know in real life. How clear our dreams and visions are depends on our power of concentration and will power. We can also use dreams to change or affect specific situations in our lives, as we saw earlier in the discussion of the power of the subconscious mind.

In order to manipulate and interpret our dreams, we must first learn the power of recollection. The jar of returning from another dimension to our own three-dimensional world (our body) usually erases any memories of all but the last few impressions of the dream world. What we must then do upon awakening is concentrate immediately on what we saw and did during the night's dreaming. Keep pencil and paper by the bed so you can write these things down in a dream diary. Frequently, of course, dreams defy words, so physical descriptions should be coupled with what you felt during the dream. An entry might look like this:

> July 12, 1984: Upon awakening at approximately 5:30 A.M.
> Thought of a dream in which I delivered two envelopes to my brother-in-law's mailbox . . . seemed important.

Before retiring, make a mental note that you wish to remember your dreams, and you will be more successful in doing so, the next morning. In one course, students are taught to put a glass of water on the night table and "program": They will drink half the water before going to bed and dreaming, and the remaining half in the morning—whereupon they will remember all they have dreamed.

DREAM INTERPRETATION

Sleep frees the subconscious mind messages that the conscious mind has kept guarded. Dreams are very complex, and analyzing them often takes a lot of work, depending on their intricacy and symbolism. Interpretation is learned through introspection, meditation, research, and practice.

Dreams are classified as either normal or psychic dreams. Most dreams are normal ones, reflecting everyday situations or thoughts, and they are often symbolic, though not psychic. They may be caused by your physical condition, strained mental activity, or stress.

For example, a man dreams of falling off a cliff and hitting the bottom of a ravine. He feels intense pain in his back. He awakens to find he has slept wrong and has a real backache. Or a woman dreams of being put in jail. In reality, she was worried about her financial situation. Or perhaps a child watches a horror movie before bedtime and dreams that monsters are trying to get him.

Psychic or supernormal dreams are caused by psychic activity received from the dreamer himself, as well as from outside sources. Sometimes the psychic dream predicts the future.

Psychic and normal dreams are experienced in much the same way. They are made up of thoughts, emotions, and sensory images. Both kinds seem real, and both can be either very fragmented or take a cohesive, storylike form. The difference is that a psychic dream contains truthful information that could not have been consciously known by the dreamer. Most dreams are a combination of psychic and normal elements, and a dream containing psychic information may, in fact, unfold in a typically normal way.

A psychic dream often is made up of symbols that seem unrelated to any of the current events of your life. The only way to recognize a dream as psychic is to recognize these symbols and wait to see if something related to them happens later. You may, in the course of dreaming, be communicating with someone. Record this information, as it may be telepathy.

The serious student who wants to learn more about the subject should look into books which deal specifically with dream interpretation. Keep in mind, though, that these books usually focus on normal, not psychic, dream interpretation. In my experience, most people seem to be better off looking within themselves for the interpretation of their dreams. If I cannot figure it out, and if there is no conscious connection, I ask my Higher Self to please reveal the message to me, in some form.

ASTRAL PROJECTION

Out-of-body experiences occur in as many as one out of three people, so they really are quite common. Usually a person is flying, falling, or floating in suspension. Following this astral journey, the person returns to his body. Often there are accompanying feelings of serenity, peace, and joy—and a desire to repeat the experience.

Here are some important facts about astral projection, or out-of-body experience:

- You have at least two guardian angels with you at all times, plus other spiritual beings to assist you in life. They also escort you out of your body and to other places on the earth plane. You can verify what you see when you return.
- Everyone moves into an OBE during sleep; people just don't remember it. Now you can direct yourself into the spirit world in your travel.
- You will be very, very conscious and aware of what you are experiencing.
- It is best to be alone when you do this, or with someone who understands what you're doing, because when you leave your physical body for this "pleasure trip" you will look somewhat lifeless and might alarm the uninformed or uneducated. Wear comfortable clothes.
- Your physical body will either breathe heavily or be in a deeply relaxed state. Your physical body will feel very little.
- The physical body sleeps, during your OBE; the mind remains totally awake.
- Have absolute trust and faith in the Supreme Force (God) and in your angels and guides.

- Don't try to deliberately leave your body if you are taking mind-altering drugs or drinking alcohol.
- There are various levels in the next dimension—from the astral levels to the highest spiritual levels. By keeping your consciousness within and attuned to God's consciousness, you will travel to the higher planes more quickly and with greater ease
- During your first out-of-body experiences, you may only float above your body or go to other places on the earth plane. Your angels and guides will want you to comfortably and gradually experience the feeling of leaving your body before you take "longer trips" that last from seconds to hours.
- When you want to return, just *think* yourself back in your body. Move your body parts.

TECHNIQUES TO HAVE AN OUT-OF-BODY EXPERIENCE

- Physical and mental relaxation is of the utmost importance. Take your time; clear your mind. No interruptions.
- Autosuggestion, self-hypnosis.
- Deep-breathing exercise.
- Meditation techniques.
- Visualization techniques: Imagine a beautiful, peaceful journey.
- Lie down and relax into the *alpha* state, but don't fall asleep. You can program your mind before sleep to travel and be aware of your journey.
- Concentrate on a spot three feet away and then gradually increase the distance. Visualize yourself (your astral self) being there.

- Affirmations: I will recall everywhere I go; I am calm; My angels and loved ones are with me; It is a joyous experience.
- Overcome fear. There may be a death fear, because separation from the physical body is much like what is expected at death. It may take repeated tries to overcome the initial fear. But don't worry—you *will* return to your body.

Chapter Three

HOW TO CHOOSE A PSYCHIC

PSYCHIC RESEARCH

According to Dr. Leonid L. Vasiliev, Chairman of Physiology at the University of Leningrad and recipient of the Lenin Prize, "The discovery of the energy underlying ESP will be equivalent to the discovery of atomic energy."

In this country, a multimillion-dollar program at Stanford Research Institute in Menlo Park, California, has been underway for more than a decade, exploring the human ability to perceive through *remote viewing*. People with this gift can experience and describe locations, events, and people at great distances—up to many thousands of miles. Some also know about events even before they happen. The concept and study of remote viewing is described in great detail by Dr. Keith Harary, in his fascinating book *The Mind Race*.

Researchers have concluded that this ability can be developed through practice. In fact, successful results were reported in twenty-six of forty-six such experiments, worldwide—suggesting that our usual perception of time and space may be terribly inaccurate.

It is difficult to say whether even more extensive testing is being conducted at governmental levels, since such projects often are listed as "classified" or masked under unlikely titles (e.g., "Novel Biological Information Transfer"). Columnist Jack Anderson, whose associates helped uncover a "psychic task force" at work in the Pentagon, estimates that our country is spending only about $6 million per year on psychic research, compared to the Russians' $30 million.

All ESP research in Russia has been government funded. Two highly respected Russian healers, Comrade Kenchadze and Colonel Alexei Krivorotov, have successfully healed back ailments, infections, and illnesses of the nervous system. Kirlian photographs showed a complete change in the energy patterns coming from Krivorotov's hands as he healed. The brightness and strength of the flares emanating from his fingers increased many times over, especially in a narrow focused channel, resembling a laser beam. The Kirlian photography also showed the changes in the amount of pain experienced by the patients.

In another experiment, Georgi Losanov of Bulgaria borrowed the Russian technique of *skin sight*—seeing by touch—conducting more than four hundred tests. He blindfolded sixty children who had been blind from birth or had gone blind in infancy. Three immediately demonstrated an innate ability to distinguish colors and geometrical figures by "skin sight." Even when the scientists hid the patterns behind glass, the youngsters could identify them. More astounding was the fact that the remaining fifty-seven children could be trained to distinguish color and pattern by feel.

Dr. Bernard Grad, of McGill University of Montreal, performed an amazing healing experiment, testing the effect a person's mental ability has on other living things around him. He proved that, if a psychic healer held a flask of water and the water later was poured onto barley seeds, the plants significantly outgrew untreated seeds. But if depressed psychiatric patients held the flask, the seeds' growth was retarded. (This will come as no surprise to those gardeners who claim that, by speaking lovingly to their plants and flowers, they get them to grow more luxuriantly and beautifully.)

Perhaps the most amazing scientific tests to date concern mental telepathy, proving that the brain's thought-energy can actually affect another person's body, physiologically. Douglas Dean, of the Newark College of Engineering, proved that when another person, across the room, sends you a telepathic message, there is actually a measurable change in *your* blood volume, even though you feel nothing.

After all these years, our logical, scientific-minded society is finally catching up with the wisdom that has existed for centuries in other parts of the world.

CHOOSING A PSYCHIC

A good psychic can make predictions in a useful way and with a high degree of accuracy. Choose the psychic and reading method best for you, but be sure to check into the psychic's professional background, paying particular attention to his or her years of experience and level of spiritual development. Ask friends you trust for their recommendations, and others you feel may be in a position to judge.

Prior to making an appointment, clarify *why* you want a reading. After making the appointment, but before you go, prepare a list of questions. Put them in the order of their importance to you, so that, if you run out of time, you have not omitted what you cared most to learn. Finally, on the day of the reading, be sure to take your list of questions and notes with you, along with any particular items you may need for your reading (a photograph or other personal object, for instance). Also take a tape recorder and blank tape, as there will be many things you will want to review later. These tapes will provide another record of your experiences and progress as you develop.

NEGATIVITY AND THE MISUSE OF PSYCHIC POWERS

Psychic ability, misunderstood by many, is not weird or strange; rather, it is completely natural, possessed in some degree by all of us, and proven throughout the ages by scholars, theologians, and scientists. Spiritual achievement is one of the most religious and holy of human endeavors, and there is no constructive use of psychic powers that can cause mental, physical, or spiritual harm.

In the course of my psychic counselings, I have met people who thought they were under psychic "attack" by demons, evil spirits, elementals, and even vampires. These things are all man-created, as *believing they exist places the image in the mind*. They are created with one's own mind energy. As I have said before, I do not believe in Satan as a little red man with a pitchfork and pointed tail. There is unquestionably a lot of negative energy in the world, and no doubt some of it may be directed toward you. If you surround yourself with good, positive people and have a happy, positive attitude, you will not attract negativity. However, remember the Law of Magnetic Attraction: Like attracts like. If you spend time in a negative environment or with negative people, you may find your own mind being swayed in a negative direction. As a result, you will begin to attract that negative energy itself.

I remember a story one woman told me about playing cards with her husband and other couples with whom they were friendly. It seems that one couple in particular always argued at the bridge table, while another treated each other with great affection and courtesy. The woman telling me her story noticed that her own husband, without even realizing it, took on the characteristics of the other men. When they played with the argumentative couple, he became sarcastic and unpleasant as well, but when they played with the others, he behaved with great kindness, mirroring the nicer men. As a result, she finally called a halt to playing with the negative couple. This confirms the old adage "The life you live is the company you keep."

There may be times, of course, when you do not have the choice of avoiding negative people. Remember, then, that through meditation and surrounding yourself with a magnetic field of white light, which no darkness can penetrate, you can protect yourself from these negative influences with your own, positive energy field. Think of God, Moses, Jesus, your angels, or whoever you feel will be uplifting to you, and ask for assistance. If you still feel this negative energy, then *command* it to leave in the name of God the Father. Another way to protect yourself is through radionics, a magnetic projection and broadcasting method widely used in Russia. This sonic device may be purchased through the mail and is legal for personal experimental purposes only.

In any case, what is most important to remember is that negative energies and thought patterns short-circuit our positive progression. The more energy taken from the negative and given to the positive, the greater the positive will become, leaving the negative to fade away from lack of energy.

Unfortunately, there will always be those who misuse their abilities to take advantage of others, and the psychic realm is no different in this regard. I recall one psychic in Fort Lauderdale, Florida, who used her gift of clairvoyance to win over the confidence of her clients, then proceeded to initiate a very expensive dependence of that person on the psychic's powers. In one case, a distraught woman had come to her, thinking there was a curse on her husband. In reality, "curses" don't exist at all. Some people can be affected by strong, negative energies directed their way, but that is not a curse *per se*. The psychic gave the woman some information about her husband which could have been obtained only through ESP and in this way won the woman's confidence. The psychic then told the client she would need to pay her several more visits, to "remove the curse." The cost was $500 per visit. Eventually, this psychic disappeared from the area and hasn't been heard from, but she may well have set up shop elsewhere, preying upon other unsuspecting clients in need.

Another example of a psychic scam involved one of my clients from Tampa. She had gone to a psychic she had read about in a local newspaper. Prior to her visit, she called and asked about the fee and was given a certain price. When she arrived for her reading, the psychic told her the "spirits" had advised him to "hold" $600 of her money, in order to accomplish her request. He assured her the money would be returned once he had solved her problem. On her next visit, he told her the spirits now said she would have to sacrifice the money. When she threatened to expose him in the press, he agreed to return the money immediately. I suggested she contact the newspaper anyway, so that other unsuspecting people would not be victimized. Scams should always be exposed, because they discredit the whole psychic field. Many supposed psychics or mentalists are actually just using magicians' techniques, and it's amazing what an expert magician can accomplish. I once attended a convention and made friends with a magician who was intrigued with what I did and asked if I was "for real." When I told him I was, I don't think he truly believed me: He had seen too many fakers to believe it could be done honestly. Later, we discussed a few "psychic" people in the public eye who he knew for a fact were using trickery. Without giving away their secrets, he explained to me how they could do what they did; it was a real eye-opener.

It is possible to tell a fake psychic from a real one, and since more and more people are entering and practicing this profession, it is important to learn how.

HOW TO DETECT A PSYCHIC SCAM

1. Check his or her credentials, degrees, media appearances, etc.

2. Before you make an appointment, check the psychic's references. Ask friends for recommendations, or check out someone who has appeared in the media.

3. Ask the psychic if you may tape the session. If the answer is "No," don't go.

4. Ask if you may bring someone along to take notes. If the psychic will not allow another person to be present, it is not a good sign.

5. Use common sense. Someone with a name such as "Sister Mother Maria Theresa" who was canonized last week by an unknown church and says she can solve all your problems is obviously a scam artist.

6. A psychic who does only past life readings isn't necessarily a fraud, but it is difficult to validate such a reading.

7. Find out if the price charged is comparable to other psychics in your area. Also, agree on the price beforehand. Be suspicious if the psychic adds on charges, changes the price, or insists on multiple visits. *Stay clear of anyone who says you have a curse or spell on you* but that, through certain rituals, they can clear it up—along with lots of your cash!

HOW I GIVE A PSYCHIC READING

I receive information in a number of ways, through clairvoyance (visual impressions), clairaudience (hearing voices and sounds), automatic writing, telepathy, and dreams.

A reading might involve one of these methods or all of them simultaneously. I touch on several areas in an individual's life: finances, travel, health, business, family, relationships, and influences surrounding the person's life. I can provide information about the subject's past, present, and future through various glimpses. We are all complex beings with a vast storehouse of information collected from our cumulative experiences, both past and present. Since the major part of your future is predestined by your own thoughts, those, too, can be tapped. However, you should remember that information on the future is not carved in stone. If your thoughts change, your future changes. No one but God knows the whole picture. I do psychic readings over the phone and through the mail just as accurately as in person.

I always inform my clients that this is how I see events and circumstances *at the time of the reading*. If I do a reading a month later, the future may have changed because of the free-will choices made by the client himself. My clients can ask questions at any point during the reading; it doesn't affect the flow of information.

It usually takes me about fifteen or twenty minutes to do a complete reading, since information is received very quickly. I don't require a specific location: A disco is as good as a quiet room, although I prefer a quiet room.

There are always opportunities and cycles in a person's life, and when I do a reading, I can see these cycles, or trends. I, like some other psychics, can see dates and times when certain opportunities may arise. By being aware of these opportunities, clients can take advantage of them more fully.

Remember, according to the Law of Cycles, you create these cycles with your thinking, which means you can speed them up or slow them down through prayer, positive programming, and meditation. This means that if I tell someone I see something happening in July and he decides to pursue it actively, it may happen in June.

People often ask me, "How can you do this over the telephone or over the radio by voice alone?" The answer is really quite simple.

I am able to tap into the God-force within, and most of the time I receive specific information with a high degree of accuracy. I continually work on my attunement—to be clearer, more defined, and accurate—through the meditation techniques I have outlined for you.

Once, while giving a lecture at the University of Miami, I was asked by a professor how I could give such simple, quick answers to very important questions without getting into heavy counseling, especially since I know people really take to heart what I say and frequently base decisions on my psychic answers. For example, a woman with marriage problems asked if she should get a divorce. I told her I didn't see the marriage working out, and that it would save her a lot of emotional strain if she were to end the marriage as soon as possible. I gave her the answer I received psychically, because that was what I felt. Had I felt there was something that could be done to save the marriage, I would have told her so. Sometimes I see difficulties ahead but feel they can be worked out. In this case I did not.

Occasionally I do get into some counseling, if I feel it is necessary. But generally, when a person comes to me, it is for a psychic answer. Based on my educational background and experience, if I feel they need psychotherapy or psychological counseling, I suggest they go to a professional in those areas.

A certain and varying percentage of my advice is just common sense, combined with my intuition and educational counseling background. Sometimes, my sessions are just "therapy" sessions, when a client wishes and needs to unload emotions and thoughts. I do whatever I can to help.

OTHER PSYCHICS

I am not perfect, nor do I make any phony, sensational claims that I know all things, can bring love back into your life, or can answer all your questions with specific details. I am not aware of any person who can do this. A person's psychic accuracy is only as clear as his attunement with the Cosmic Intelligence and his ability to be a clear channel. Since man is limited by the confines of a body which, in turn, is affected by his total environment (health, other people, distractions, state of mind, etc.), he cannot be a perfect, pure, clear channel of God's information. With man's limitations on understanding, pure information would be too complex and abstract for us to comprehend.

If the spiritual pipeline gets clogged with distractions, negative people, ill health, etc., then it will be difficult to receive clear, intuitive information. It is a continual process to keep it clear and clean through meditation, prayer, and following the Golden Rule. No one can receive *all* information. No psychic can say he or she is the best in the world. Traveling the country, I am amused to hear psychics say they are "Number One." Being well known doesn't mean a psychic is the best.

In a recent case, a group of well-known psychics got together to help the police find a missing child. Ultimately, the body was found, but it was nowhere near where the psychic search took place. Even all these well-known and well-intentioned psychics didn't come close to locating the child. Rae Graham, the white woman witch doctor/Western-trained nurse mentioned earlier, says the witch doctors are accurate about 70 percent of the time—roughly the same, she says, as Western-trained physicians.

When you walk into a grocery store and pick up a supermarket tabloid that lists "great psychics' predictions," the headlines seem very impressive. However, studies have shown that the vast majority of these predictions never come true. The prediction listed in the tabloid may, in fact, be one that did come true—fifteen or twenty years ago!

Psychics can hit on certain areas that are accurate, but if you put ten of the world's supposed best in a room and ask the same question of all of them, perhaps one will get the answer. Some or one of them might get an answer similar to the correct one—as, for instance, if a person's name was Janice and a psychic got the letter J but said Jane, Janet, or Jan. To a skeptic, that might seem like guessing, while to a believer in ESP it would be considered a good answer. Remember, no one is a perfectly clear channel receiving all exact information.

There is no way to determine the ranks of the world's foremost psychics. Those who test accurately under laboratory conditions with playing cards may not accurately be able to tune into a person's life, and vice versa.

To determine a percentage of accuracy, you would need to take one hundred people and give them readings broken into three basic areas: past, present, and future. Then ask each psychic specific questions for each area. You could determine immediately the accuracy for the past and present, but for the future, you would need to trace the subjects for another twenty years. Future accuracy will always be less than that of the past and present because of the free will choices the subjects make, now and in the future.

I know of no psychic (myself included) who could pass a skeptic's test in which a psychic is asked questions about a group of people, such as "What is this person's mother's name?" "Where does that man live?" "What is the name of this person's street?" etc. That simply cannot be done consistently without some form of trickery. As I've said before, we all possess these powers to some degree, so why should we rely on someone else to tell us things we can find out for ourselves, using our own intuitive abilities? A good spiritual psychic should be regarded as an adept and sympathetic counselor. Psychological dependence on a psychic can develop in the same way as dependence on a psychiatrist. Remember that, as with so many skills possessed by humans, not all psychics' powers are equal. The final analysis of how good a psychic is will always be how accurate he or she is.

HOW YOU CAN GIVE A PSYCHIC READING

You have learned who God is, as a power and as an intelligence (not a man), that He is always with you, and that you have angels and other spiritual representatives assisting you. You have also learned about the power of prayer, the importance of your awareness of the white light of spiritual protection, and how to read an aura. You have come to understand what a psychic impression is, why and how to meditate, and the proper breathing techniques that relax you and improve the spiritual flow. And, in addition, you have experienced the channeling of energy while practicing healing. Now that you've learned all these basic steps, you are ready to do a "reading" for someone else.

It is best to do this for someone you do not know, so you won't have any preconceived ideas. Or ask a friend about someone you don't know and to tell you only this person's name and age. Through your friend, you can verify the psychic information you receive. Try to answer questions such as these:

1. What does he look like?
2. Is he single, married, or divorced?
3. Does he live in a house, townhouse, or apartment?
4. Does he have a car? What kind? Color?
5. Does he have any pets? What kind? Color?
6. What is his favorite food?
7. What is his favorite color?
8. Give three names you see close around him.
9. What does he do for a living?

10. Is he basically a happy person, or does he tend to be
    more negative and miserable?

During the reading, remain relaxed and comfortable. Do not allow yourself to get tense. If you do, then stop and take deep breaths, to regain a more relaxed state.

All the information you want is there and available through the universal force. *You* are the only block to receiving it. You *will* get an answer. Don't be afraid if it is wrong. Even if you get none, or only one, right at first, it's a beginning—and the more you do, the more accurate you will become.

You may wonder how much of the information is just a guess and how much is psychic. Remember, as I mentioned earlier, when talking about discernment, through time and practice you will come to *know*.

The most important aspect of practicing is the accuracy of the information you receive about *yourself*. Ask questions of yourself. When you have a problem, look to yourself, first, for the answer. Let's say you have three job offers. Tune in to feel which is the best. If you are dating someone you really like, but things aren't going well, try stepping out of your emotional shell to find the answer. Don't be afraid of what you will discover. Ask that the truth of the situation be revealed to you. It is always better to know and be prepared, so you can protect yourself from further heartache.

It is also helpful, when developing your psychic ability, to be around someone more psychic than yourself. Just as in sports, it helps to advance your own ability. Bob came to me for a consultation. He didn't think he had any psychic ability. In fact, he never had even considered it. Now, after a few years, Bob has turned into an excellent psychic. He's not interested in doing it professionally; he just wants to receive information for his friends, his loved ones, and himself. He was always a very spiritual person and became extremely good at creativity visualizing situations. He began simply by following my psychic and spiritual development and programming techniques, along with his own intuition, and he has had amazing results.

FREE WILL AND PREDESTINATION

Most people define *free will* as the freedom to do or say anything we want to. Most (Americans!) also agree this is a God-given right. In fact, free will governs our whole life.

The important thing is not so much what you believe but the intentions and motives behind your thoughts and actions. You may hear a religious fanatic say his belief is the only true one, and that if you don't believe his way, you'll go to hell. This is not the case. If you truly believe in your own convictions (regardless of what they are and as long as you are not hurting anyone), God will see your sincere intentions and will not punish you for your beliefs. We all operate on different levels, in our transition from earthly beings to divine beings. This is part of God's divine plan. Indeed, most people are proud of their individuality and praise it in others. So, if you've ever asked yourself why there are so many diverse religions, each with its own advocates, the answer is *free will*.

Some people consider astrology their religion, but I believe they look at astrological charts the wrong way. The locations of the planets at the time and location of your birth surely influence and affect your life. But to read a newspaper column every day and follow its advice completely is sheer folly. The best and most competent of astrologers emphasize the *influence* of the planets, not the tyranny: The power of your free will is so strong it can overcome any obstacle.

PREDESTINATION

A lot is written about predestination, but *we create our destinies with our minds*. Our choices determine how far we will progress.

When a psychic gives a reading about a person's future, the psychic information is used as a tool to reach the person's mind. For example, if I get an impression that your car will have brake failure, what I'm really saying is that I know it will happen *if you don't get the brakes fixed*. Or if I see an opportunity opening for you that you should take advantage of, you are then free to take my advice or not, according to your own free will. Each of us receives messages telling us what we already know is right or wrong. We enjoy or suffer the consequences of the decisions *we* make based on those messages. Using free will to its fullest advantage, then, means using your own psychic intuition to guide your life.

I do not believe the theory that our days are numbered and that, no matter what we do, we'll still die at a given time. I put forth all the effort I can to achieve my goals. I try to follow all the holistic principles I've outlined in this book and work diligently to minimize my risks. When I drive, I wear a seat belt, totally disagreeing with those "fatalists" who say, "Why should I wear a seat belt? If my time is up, there's nothing I can do about it, and I'm going to die."

Only after I do everything in my power to make my life safe, successful, and happy—*then and only then*—can I tell God that I've done my very best, always putting my life in His hands. Then I can comfortably say, "What will be will be. If it is His will that I pass on tomorrow, then I will do so knowing that it is in my highest and best interest. But *I do not intend to have my life end by any careless mistake on my part.*

Part Four

RELATIONSHIPS
AND SEX

There are people who take the heart out of you, and there
are people who put it back.
—ELIZABETH DAVID

Keep away from people who try to belittle your ambition.
Small people always do that, but the really great make you
feel that you, too, can become great.
—MARK TWAIN

Mark them who cause divisions and offenses, and avoid
them.
—ROMANS 16:17

Many waters cannot quench love, neither can the floods
drown it.
—SONG OF SOLOMON 8:7

Whether man associates with a good man or bad, with a
thief or an ascetic, he undergoes their influence, as cloth
that of the dye.
—MAHABHARATA 5.36,13.10

Chapter One

LOVE RELATIONSHIPS

As you are a direct reflection of your environment, and your environment a reflection of you, so your attitudes, the people around you, and your relationships affect and are affected by your holistic health.

In the past twenty-five years, millions of people have attended workshops and seminars dedicated to Finding the Real You or to Looking Out for Number One. For many, such sessions were a positive turning point in their lives; for others, they did nothing more than encourage self-centeredness and greed at the expense of others. When every person expresses himself so openly, a clash of values is inevitable. Remember the classic television series *All in the Family?* The differences between Archie and his daughter and son-in-law caused constant turmoil. Archie's conservative, racist, and close-minded attitude against the children's more liberal and often radical lifestyle made their home a battlefield. It may have been funny to watch on television, but living that sort of life is far from amusing.

As you grow into higher consciousness, you will discover that it is more important to *be* the right person than to *find* the right person. This follows the Universal Law of Attraction ("Like attracts like"). Opposites may attract initially, but rarely do they remain together. It is one thing to believe that people seek those who "complete" them by providing strengths they do not have, but a difference in values, standards, and vision will cause little but strife.

All relationships affect your health and well-being. Another person's vibrations can upset or complement your own. Avoid close ties with anyone on a lower vibrancy level than your own. It is sometimes difficult to categorize vibratory levels except by your own intuitive feelings, but since the discovery of the Kirlian photography process, we can actually watch those levels change with certain behaviors. For example, smoking, drinking alcohol, and negative thoughts appear as dimming, shrinking or a breaking in the aura. Even positive people who take care of their health find that associating with negative/low-vibrational people takes it toll. Those who are unhappy, depressed, negative, sick, bored, or constantly fatigued affect the physical and mental state of those around them. On the other hand, you may have heard someone say, of an attractive person, "Her laughter is infectious" or "Her smile lights up any room," proving the old adage, "The life you lead is the company you keep."

A WELL-BALANCED RELATIONSHIP

Being the right person means being a *whole person,* first, before becoming involved in a relationship. *Whole* means not being dependent upon anyone or anything to make you happy and complete. You may say, "All I need to be happy is to become president of this corporation. Nothing else matters." Or, "When I find the perfect mate, all my problems will be solved." But really, the only true happiness comes in accepting and being content with yourself and your life. No one could ever have enough money, power, or prestige to fill the void of discontent. That emotion will never be fulfilled, because fulfillment comes not from *external* circumstances, but from *within.* As some have put it, you must be *cause,* not *effect.* You are a choicemaker, not a victim of circumstances. Remember that you always have the option of making changes in your life to become a happier, more satisfied person. If you *think* happy and healthy, you will *be* happy and healthy.

Choosing to become whole means getting in touch with yourself and your needs and learning to love yourself completely, knowing that God loves you completely. Know that, in His eyes, you are perfect now, but that if you choose to be more prosperous, loving, or even more humorous, it is within your power to be so.

When you are in total harmony with yourself, you will be amazed at the good things that happen to you. Once you are a happy, whole, loving person, you are ready to attract a happy, whole, loving mate. If you choose as a partner someone who is similar to yourself, he or she will be an extension of your happiness, as you will be of his or hers.

No relationship can be satisfactory if the partners are dependent on each other to make them feel loved, respected, and worthwhile. These qualities come when you are in touch with yourself and the God-force within you. Holistic love should be accepted for as long as it lasts, whether two months or ten years. Do not enter into it expecting guarantees that it will last forever.

Be aware that you are constantly growing and changing, and that is true of everyone. Make note of your growth patterns, including the cycles of love, finances, and health. Knowing the direction and growth in different areas of your life—and in the life of your partner—can help you better deal with any relationship. Those who grow together stay together. Many marriage breakups are the result of ignoring such patterns. If you are growing into a more loving, spiritual person while your mate is moving toward alcoholism, it's obviously not going to work. Likewise, if you are very ambitious but your mate wants you to stay home all the time and keep him company in front of the television set, there certainly will be complications.

Communication—talking, listening, and *hearing*—remains the best way to deal with such situations. If you are happy, your mate is more likely to be happy. Talk together about your mutual desires, interests, and plans. Discuss your expectations, morals, and limitations. As author Douglas Steere writes, in *A Random Harvest,* "To 'listen' another's soul into a condition of disclosure and discovery may be almost the greatest service that any human being ever performs for another."

Be honest, and listen to your mate's needs. Don't assume your loved one automatically knows what you want and need, or can read your mind. And don't play games: *That's* not fair to either of you.

Certain qualities are present in any well-balanced relationship. Among these are friendship, respect, and encouragement.

It is important to be each other's best friend. Enjoying each other's company and spending time together laughing, sharing, and stimulating each other intellectually, spiritually, and physically with affection and tenderness, can make a love relationship work.

Always have respect for one another's opinions, intellect, reaction, business and religious beliefs. This doesn't mean you must agree on everything, but show a willingness to "walk in the other person's moccasins." Be considerate and appreciative of what your partner is and does.

Have faith in your loved ones and confidence in their integrity, without suspicion. And be honest in return, to have that trust reciprocated. It is important to be able to trust what your mate will say *and* do.

Give support and inspiration to the people you love, so they will feel happy and motivated. Sincere encouragement helps us to grow and evolve to our fullest potential. Take pride in your partner and in what he or she does. And always remember that "a man doesn't have to extinguish another man's candle to make his own shine brighter."

Drs. Marguerite and Marshall Shearer describe a "Ladder of Love" that has seven rungs. As they explain, people generally take the best relationship they know as their definition of love, but the "upright parts of the ladder are self-respect and respect for the partner. These need to be approximately equal for a relationship to endure." The rungs of their ladder are these:

RECOGNITION: The lowest rung on the ladder makes you feel special. Being ignored or treated as a nonperson is the worst put-down of all.

NEGATIVE ATTENTION: At least it's better than being ignored. A child who has to attract a parent's attention by getting into some kind of trouble is apt to create problems in a grown-up relationship.

POSITIVE ATTENTION: Being there. Listening.

ACCEPTANCE: Accepting another person just the way he or she is. No conditions.

OPPORTUNITY TO GIVE: Having something to give. Having a value other than always being on the receiving end.

ADMIRATION: Admiring another person without putting yourself down.

PSYCHOLOGICAL INTIMACY: The top rung on the ladder. Sharing hopes, dreams, and aspirations. Exposing weaknesses and being open.

The doctors (she, a former family practitioner; he, a psychiatrist) add, finally, "We believe love is caring as much about the other person's happiness as you care about your own in day-to-day living. And sometimes even more."

Have you ever noticed how people who are in love actually seem to "glow"? This is why it is true that all brides are beautiful— even those not beautiful by any of the usual aesthetic standards. Scientists have discovered that smiles, laughter, and feelings of love actually release beneficial hormones, while frowns and anger release negative, destructive ones. The beneficial hormones make us radiant and, in turn, the radiance releases more of those same, life-enhancing hormones. We have known for some time that people who live alone live longer and happier lives when they have pets they love, proving the *physical,* as well as *emotional* benefits of caring deeply for someone or something. (In cases where pets are not wanted or practical, a keen concern for a given *cause* will have the same result. It is simply important to have an interest in something other than oneself.)

The ideal love relationship combines all the important elements of life. It is multidimensional. A moving example of such a relationship was revealed in the words spoken by Maurice Tempelsman, longtime companion of Jacqueline Kennedy Onassis, at Jackie's funeral. Describing their life together, he said, " . . . It was filled with adventure and wisdom, laughter and love, gallantry and grace." One cannot help but recognize, from those few words, the very special quality of what they shared.

THE FIVE TYPES OF LOVE

There are five types of love: *physical* (sexual), *spiritual* (divine, nonsexual, cosmic, unconditional, all-encompassing), *mental* (intellectual), *emotional* (intense feelings), and *holistic* (all of the above).

A holistic love relationship is stimulating physically, mentally, emotionally, and spiritually, and it is by far the most lasting kind of relationship. When two spiritually minded individuals fall in love, the result is a much more fulfilling experience than is possible with just physical and emotional love.

God's love is eternal. Ideally, to receive love is to give with no thought of return. To love unselfishly is its own reward. This is the concept taught by Jesus. Even if your love is not returned, it will not be wasted; rather, it will flow right back into your own heart. Therefore, never be afraid to love.

The joy of any love surely will disappear if it becomes obsessive, addictive, and/or dependent. Love often becomes an addiction like alcohol or drugs. In insecure people it manifests itself as a craving for approval, affection, and constant companionship. It can interfere with one's ability to function at work and in social situations. Acute withdrawal symptoms, such as altered eating and sleeping patterns, occur when such dependent relationships come to an end. These are signs of depression and are a common reaction in cases of loss.

Rudolf Steiner illustrates different relationships through the use of circles. The two circles in figure A, below, represent two unre-

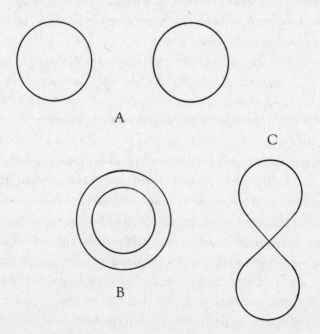

lated individuals at the beginning of a relationship. Figure B represents one of the individuals trying to dominate, control, ridicule, or usurp the position of the other. (This domination may be subtle or overt.) At that point, the weaker person begins to lose his or her freedom and individuality and is submerged into or absorbed by the stronger one. This is an unhealthy relationship. An ideal relationship is shown in figure C. The two individuals complement, enrich, and fulfill each other. Each must be on equal ground. Here there is a flow between the two lives, with each retaining individuality and freedom. This is the type of relationship often described as "not two people facing each other all the time but, rather, holding hands and walking in the same direction, together."

It is possible to love different people in vastly different ways. Some relationships are just physical, others mental or spiritual. Remember that not all relationships are meant to last forever. God always know why someone is not right for you. Pay attention to Him: He wants you to learn from all your experiences. Be strong and know that better circumstances lie ahead.

Relationships also can be complementary. A variety of people can fill dimensions in your life that are not taken care of by your main love relationship. You can love more than one person at a time, but it is rare to be *in love* with more than one at a time.

Yale psychologist Dr. Robert Sternberg concluded, in a recent study, that three main ingredients are necessary for a successful long-term love relationship: passion, intimacy, and commitment. All relationships go through trying times. Your ability to deal with the problems that arise is a direct reflection of your inner strength. Do not subject yourself to unreasonable difficulties, but assess the positives and negatives when major problems arise. Although physical abuse, constant arguing, and continuing infidelity are destructive to a relationship and legitimate reasons for terminating it, even these problems may be resolved under certain circumstances.

HOW TO ATTRACT THE IDEAL MATE

If you would like to attract the ideal mate, focus your attention on that part of your life and adapt your Future Plan and Future Plan Scrapbook by adding more specifics:

- Write in your Future Plan all the qualities you seek in a mate.
- Update your scrapbook. Create a page on each individual quality and add a picture which expresses it. Add pictures of where you'd like to go and what you'd like to do.
- Visualize pleasing scenes with your ideal person in your mind. See that person sitting on your sofa, making you dinner, or smiling at you. Visualize what makes you happy and content.
- Affirm that God, working through your subconscious mind, will bring your ideal mate into your life in divine order. Know that, if there is no one in your life right now, there is a reason. You should use this time constructively. Don't just pine away waiting for someone to enter your life. Join clubs, socialize with friends, go to a festival or to sporting events. Getting out and doing something worthwhile can be very gratifying. You can share your love with others by becoming a volunteer. Try being a Big Brother or Big Sister, helping the handicapped, or working with animals.

Always keep in mind the Law of Magnetic Attraction. Remember that what and whom you seek is seeking you with equal intensity. Also remember that "like attracts like": If you want someone honest, be honest. You don't have to be wealthy to attract someone wealthy, but be sure to have a wealthy attitude, not a poverty mentality.

As you show faith in what you're doing and continue with a positive, helpful attitude, you will be amazed at how quickly things begin to happen. Your ideal mate will come into your life in no time! This actually happened to me, so I know it works. I was visualizing and writing down my goals and had decided I wanted to meet a man like one I had seen on the cover of a catalog. One day, I met a man who seemed kind and intellectual, and I agreed to have dinner with him. I noticed how he resembled the man in the catalog but didn't really give it much thought. He was visiting Fort Lauderdale, where I met him, and later—on a table at his hotel—I saw the same catalog I had at home. I casually mentioned that I had the same catalog and, just as casually, he replied, "That's me on the cover"!

Once again, remember the importance to a relationship of similar goals, ambitions, and energy levels. You want to feel like part of the same team, not like antagonists or competitors.

LOVE CYCLES

Relationships, according to the Law of Cycles, last a finite length of time. Each one, whether friendship or love relationship, might be ideal for six months or sixty years; then the cycle might change. Enjoy a person for however long the relationship lasts—usually the length of the love cycle. If you are a whole person, you will emerge from the experience still a whole person, but one more evolved and ready for your next period of growth. If one partner has grown faster than the other, the breakup may be not only inevitable but desirable.

EXPECTATIONS

Often, we expect too much from one person; we should be more re-alistic in our expectations. Each of us, at any given time, has something valuable to offer, and everything in life is an exchange. These exchanges can take place at a number of levels, and we shouldn't judge one person's strengths or gifts as being better than another's. An intuitive and sensitive person can benefit from the analytical mind of his or her partner, and their relationship can thrive on the synergism. If you accurately and honestly assess the person with whom you are involved, you will be able to be more accepting. In this way you both will avoid the unhappiness, depression, and frustration brought on by disappointment.

Fort Lauderdale psychologist Dr. Fay Mitchell describes what happens more often than not. "When you meet somebody, you set up unspoken rules. If you're going to give, give, give, then the rules have been set up that you're the giver and the other person is the taker. When you first meet you must make sure you're not the giver constantly, because at some point you may suddenly change and say you don't want these rules. The other person hasn't changed; you have. You've decided to change the rules in the middle of the game. This is the point where a lot of relationships go down the drain."

By talking and spending time with the other person, you will receive cues about your future life together. According to Dr. Mitchell, "The person may be saying that he or she is ambitious or something of that nature, but most people pay no attention to those cues. Sometimes you're so caught up in the situation that, although you listen, you don't hear. Later, disillusionment sets in."

Never go into a relationship or marriage with the idea of changing the other person. You choose to be with that person be-cause of who and what he or she is *now*. Chances are, no change will take place. The exception, of course, occurs when a person makes a personal commitment to change. But that commitment cannot be coerced. It must come from within, and from a deep desire.

MARRIAGE

Marriage is a changing institution. In the past, many marriages were arranged by relatives or set up for financial reasons. Today most people decide to marry for emotional reasons. The old marriage structure, in which the husband goes to work while the wife remains home to raise and watch the children is rapidly giving way to double-career families, often with no children at all. (The term DINKs was coined to describe a marriage in which there is <u>D</u>ouble <u>I</u>ncome, <u>N</u>o <u>K</u>ids.) Today, wives have more freedom to leave an unhappy situation because they no longer are dependent solely on their husbands for support. In addition, divorce has become more widely accepted. It is interesting to note that most divorced people don't have negative feelings about the institution of marriage: Seventy-five to eighty percent of them remarry.

I think people often break up because they are searching only for romance. They expect their own relationship to be the same as those they see on the screen, in books, and in ads. Marriages built on these unrealistic expectations cannot and do not last very long.

Marriages are not all made in heaven. In fact, God is not responsible at all for our feelings and misfortunes. He did not put us on earth to follow some predetermined pattern laid out by Him, but rather to use our free will and take responsibility for our actions. When a person goes through the marriage ceremony, the words *Whom God has joined let no man put asunder,* do not mean that God has selected these two people as lifelong mates. A religious officiator may give the impression that God has sanctioned the marriage, but this is not the case. Man chooses woman; woman chooses man. It is your decision what you do with your life. If a marriage ends in divorce, the couple still has learned an enormous amount from the experience.

One of the most important factors in choosing a mate is spirituality. Both partners should be at the same, or nearly the same, spiritual development level. To truly know a person, meditate and pray with him. Ask for divine guidance. If you are meant to be together, you will find out. If you are not destined to stay together, don't be afraid. Releasing can be difficult, but we must learn to let go emotionally, mentally, physically, and spiritually. Request that God bring you someone better, if this person is not right for you. Trust your situation to God, knowing that He will always fill your needs. A spiritual counselor, priest, or rabbi may also be helpful.

Most relationships begin on the physical level, then, if all goes well, develop to the mental and emotional level of development. Unfortunately, few people reach the spiritual stage or even realize that it exists and is necessary. But the more aware a person is, the more discriminating he or she can be about the areas of a relationship which need attention.

I have never been married, not because I am opposed to marriage but simply because, even having dated a wide variety of men, I have never met the right, holistic person. I continue to meditate and pray with the affirmation in mind that who and what I am seeking is seeking me with equal intensity.

MARRIAGE CYCLES

Even permanent relationships go through cycles, and knowing about cycles can help you work through them. Psychologists recognize that "the two-year *hitch*, the seven-year *itch*, and the seventeen-to-twenty-year *ditch*" are typical marriage cycles.

The "two-year hitch" is a period of adjustment. If the individuals involved don't adjust well to each other in that period of time, there could be a separation. At the seven-year point the couples may become bored and one of the partners may decide to look for more excitement by having an affair. The "seventeen-to-twenty-year ditch" generally occurs after the children have finished school or left home and the parents look at each other and wonder what they really have in common anymore. Frequently they find they only stayed together for the children and that they hardly even know each other.

It is important that parents spend time alone together each day, without the distractions of business or children. Each partner should ask and listen to what the other has done that day, so they continue to grow *together*, instead of apart. I once heard a woman tell others around her that, every evening when her husband came home, they went into their den and closed the door and spent his first hour at home just being with each other. No children could interrupt; no phone calls were answered. The other women were stunned that she could be so selfish and would "close her children out." Many years later, when a number of the other women in the crowd had long since been divorced, this woman and her husband still enjoyed themselves and each other, and their children were happy, functioning adults with their own equally independent children.

Sometimes, career and health cycles play havoc with a marriage. People grow at different speeds, weaving in and out of cycles at varying times. If one partner has difficulties adapting, major conflicts can result. For example, a man with a demanding career is married to a woman who stays home to raise the children. A few years later, the man decides he wants to cut back and focus more attention on his family. But by now the woman, who has been home with the children all these years, wants to get out into the world and expand her own horizons. If her husband insists she stay home with him, a conflict in cycles might arise.

In another situation, the woman has stayed home with the children and has had very little outside activity for herself, but the man has been thriving on the business and social aspects of his life. He's been meeting new people and learning new things. Suddenly, he looks at his wife and thinks she's dull. There is a good chance she's not much different intellectually from when they first met and married, but the man has changed. He has grown, while she has been limited to the confines of the household. In either of these situations, the couple may face a common problem: One of the partners decides to have an extramarital affair.

EXTRAMARITAL AFFAIRS

While it may appear that man (and woman) is a polygamous creature because of the number of people who have extramarital affairs or multiple relationships, it is not that we were born to be polygamous but, rather, that we become that way while searching for the perfect person. Everyone is looking for Mr. or Ms. Right. If two people are truly satisfied and have made the correct choice, they probably will not look elsewhere. But that doesn't mean they won't admire or feel affection for other people. That is a natural state of affairs.

Those who are not holistically compatible continue their search for the right person, even when that means hurting the person with whom they are involved. If you know you are hurting someone by having an affair, you will produce bad karma.

An affair my be the *symptom* of a failing relationship or a *warning* that your marriage could use some reevaluation. It is not always an indication that the marriage is over. Many married couples stay together for years after an affair is over and done with, and some are actually made better and stronger because of it. Sometimes such seemingly bad circumstances serve to open a dialogue that, otherwise, would never have been attempted. It takes a great deal of willingness and commitment to continue a relationship after such a break, but two determined and sincere partners can make anything happen together.

FALLING OUT OF LOVE

Falling *in* love can be the most exciting thing in a person's life. Falling *out* of love often can be the most difficult. Since love is not a rational feeling, it is virtually impossible to reason those love feelings away. As the seventeenth-century French philosopher Pascal said, "The heart has its reasons which Reason doesn't know." Learning to deal with the loss of a love is the key to returning to a happy state of mind.

Along with your meditation, prayers, and positive thinking, there are other key techniques that can bring you back to your normal, healthy state. An excellent book on the subject is *How to Fall Out of Love,* by Dr. Debora Phillips, in which the behavior therapist examines and explains what have been her patients' most successful behavior patterns.

One technique described by Dr. Phillips is *thought-stopping*, developed by Dr. Joseph Wolpe, Professor of Psychiatry at the Temple University School of Medicine. In thought-stopping, a person suppresses the thought of the other person at the very minute it begins, replacing it with a pleasant thought. If thinking about lying on a beach in Hawaii gets your mind off the person you're trying to forget, then think about Hawaii. By doing this, you will think of the person less often.

Another technique is called *positive image building*. This includes praising yourself, using thought-stopping techniques when a self-critical or depressing thought enters your mind; practicing being assertive; allowing yourself to be self-indulgent; and using positive reinforcement. In other words, positive image building means congratulating yourself on a job well done. This confirms the validity of the Yale study on the Psychology of Love, in which it was found that one of the major factors in the poor choice of partners is low self-esteem. Those who feel they must always prove their worth or value to another tend to choose partners who take advantage of them. Those with greater self-esteem *know* their value and choose partners who recognize and appreciate it.

DIVORCE

I believe that God does want everyone to be content. If a marriage is an unhappy situation, the union should be dissolved. Divorce, however, is viewed in many ways, and marriage counseling should always be sought prior to instituting divorce proceedings. It is extremely helpful to have someone else mediate your problems. Divorce should be the final choice, after all other attempts to work things out together have failed, or if there is physical, mental, or emotional abuse in the relationship. Never stay with anyone out of fear.

If you have decided on a course of divorce, make every effort to accomplish it quickly and with as little rancor as possible. The bitterness of divorce can poison your thoughts for years to come, if you allow it to. But if you remember to send blessings and love to those who have harmed and hurt you, your own growth will occur more rapidly and completely, and you can begin to build a new life for yourself, full of your fondest dreams and desires. Remember, too, to thank and praise God for your mistakes and difficulties and to ask his assistance in guiding you on a better path.

ENVIRONMENT AND AFFECTION

You are probably aware by now that with the physical relationship you choose, you are subconsciously creating an environment similar to the one in which you yourself were raised. We recreate that which is most familiar to us, whether good or bad. Research has shown that those raised in an unaffectionate family often subconsciously choose an unaffectionate partner. Children who were frequently abused subconsciously seek abusive mates or become abusive parents. Children of alcoholic parents find themselves married to alcoholics or become alcoholics themselves. (This was the basic concept of Deborah Norwood's book *Women Who Love Too Much*.)

It follows, then, that those brought up in affectionate families are generally affectionate themselves. They expect their relationships to be loving, appreciative, and communicative. Affectionate people who marry unaffectionate people may find a great deal of strain and dissatisfaction in the relationship. Psychological counseling can help those who desire it to become more openly affectionate. Just as studies have shown that even plants grow more luxuriant when openly shown care and affection by those cultivating them, so a love relationship will thrive and grow when open, frequent, and sincere caring and affection is expressed by each of the partners.

Chapter Two

SEXUAL RELATIONSHIPS

If you are a sexually active person, you should most likely seek a mate who shares the same desires. If you aren't very much interested in sex, you may find yourself unhappy with someone whose needs are noticeably greater. Partners with divergent sexual needs often find that these differences affect the rest of the relationship as well.

Sexual compatibility is not only physical but should involve emotional, mental, and spiritual attunement. This is holistic sex. Sexual intercourse, in its most basic form, is nothing more than an exercise leading to ejaculation or orgasm and creating a sense of release. A sexual experience that is emotional and mental is very fulfilling. But the orgasm which occurs when two holistic people make love transcends pure physical release and even goes beyond the emotional/mental level, resulting in a more spiritually energizing and emotionally satisfying encounter between two truly compatible people. After sharing a holistic orgasm, a person feels elevated and satisfied, as opposed to the fatigue and, sometimes, slight depression one may feel after a purely physical encounter. (Although the sexual act itself may be enjoyable, many people—especially those engaging in "recreational sex"—report an emotional letdown once the act is complete.)

I do not believe that those who choose homosexual relationships are committing a spiritual sin. I know this often is a religious issue, but I don't see how sexual preferences have anything to do with a person's spiritual evolution. I believe that God understands those who choose this kind of relationship. Studies have shown that homosexuality stems from a complex set of biological, cultural, and environmental circumstances.

Neither do I believe that premarital sex is a sin. To me, it doesn't damage one's relationship with God. Promiscuity, on the other hand, can be damaging both physically and spiritually. Obsession with anything on the physical plane takes away from commitments to other aspects of life and to spiritual growth, and the dangers of sexually transmitted disease make this kind of behavior life threatening to both the individual and his or her whole family. Increasingly, the clergy of a wide range of religions and denominations are dealing with sex between mature, committed adults who— for whatever reason—are not married, as an important part of their counseling.

SEXUAL MISCONCEPTIONS

A large number of people have misconceptions and fears about sex: fears of being used or abused sexually, fears about not being able to perform well or to reach orgasm, misconceptions about what sex is and what it should mean in their lives. Sometimes these fears and confusion block sexual energy, causing needs to go unmet. When the needs for caring, tenderness, and total body involvement are not met, you may find yourself disappointed and frustrated, leading to a damaged self-concept. This can be detrimental to your holistic health, although an active sex life is not necessarily important to maintain good physical health. In other words, it is not the presence or absence of sex that counts in a relationship but rather the accompanying feelings and behavior.

Society has led us to develop unrealistic expectations about how great sex is supposed to be and how it can solve all our problems. When sex is described as ecstasy, or as the ultimate achievement, we are bound to feel inadequate when our own experiences fall short. Many problems also arise from the feeling that sex is something dirty or an act to be feared, earned, or supplied on demand. Such guilt and lack of understanding may foster a fear of the body in general. Myths and some religions have long presented masturbation as abnormal, unnatural, antisocial, and physically harmful. In truth, self-initiated pleasure is quite natural and is one of the finest ways of developing your sexual awareness. There should be no guilt associated with experiencing this joy. Guilt and confusion in this area may result in a mental blocking of sexual energy, causing problems like frigidity.

ORGASM AND SEX

Both men and women have difficulty achieving orgasm, frequently as a result of psychological factors. Usually, a woman relates to a man in a way similar to the one in which she related to her father or to other male authority figures in her life. If she learned to be generally responsive to him, she will be better able to respond psychologically and sexually to other men in her life.

The inability to discuss sexual feelings and preferences, or the mistaken belief that sex is dirty or sinful, can result in reduced sexual pleasure or difficulty in "letting go" and achieving orgasm. The inability to relax, overtiredness, malnutrition, or illness also can interfere, as will fears of pregnancy or disease. Psychologically and emotionally, a sense of complete trust on the part of both partners will increase the pleasure immeasureably; a lack of trust can destroy that pleasure.

Although a number of *physical* factors causing impotence have recently been documented, it is more often than not the psychological factors that impede a man's ability to perform. His relationship with his mother or with other close female figures in his life often determines his attitude toward women later on. The fear of failure to perform or to satisfy his partner is a major problem for some men; in others, tension in the back, pelvis and legs can cause premature ejaculation. Often, a "poor performance" is the result of nothing more than a lack of experience. As with most problems, practice and a positive outlook on life help greatly, as will a loving and understanding partner.

In mature adults (as opposed to hormonally active adolescents) sex is a complex activity involving much more than the physical act. Intercourse is not making love, and making love is not just intercourse. The most rewarding sex act always involves positive feelings and emotions; it involves all the senses influenced by your inner thoughts and it involves your ability to communicate with yourself and your partner. Sex is a communion with another human being—a communion of your body, mind, and spirit. One can be satisfied physically, yet still long for missing emotional support and love.

Sex can and should be a truly satisfying and fulfilling pleasure in your life. It is part of your divine being as well as your physical self. Accepting and sharing this pleasure with someone for whom you care deeply is like celebrating the magnificent creature you are. As a child you naturally played with your body. You enjoyed the freedom of nakedness and took open pleasure in being held against the bodies of others, being stroked and gently tickled. There was no shame or fear attached to any of these pleasures until others told you you were too old for those things. In this way, children grow to think that what feels good to them is unacceptable to others. To enjoy sex to its fullest, as an adult, means to revert to a playful, childlike state of simply knowing what naturally feels good to you and doing it.

An important step in awareness is realizing that your mind is probably your most potent sexual device. In fact, it has been said that "the largest sexual organ in the body is the brain." Be aware of your thoughts, and think about the things you want to happen in your life. Think positively, as that puts you in a better frame of mind and contributes to improving your sexual pleasure. Whatever thoughts you have, your body follows. If preoccupations during sex take your mind off sexuality, your body will react accordingly. Thinking about a problem at the office will distract you from your sexual partner and make you lose the intensity needed to have a fulfilling experience. Likewise, fear can freeze your satisfaction, just as guilt and anxiety can stifle your pleasure. Be aware of your thoughts and inner dialogue, so that—if your mind starts to wander—you can gently bring your awareness back to the part of the body being touched. Bring yourself back to the here and now. Breathe deeply and allow the feelings of arousal to spread throughout your body, opening all your sensory pathways. This will increase your pleasure many times over and—through synergy—the pleasure of your partner, as well.

You are the expert on yourself. Take responsibility and decide what you like and what you don't like. Learn that you have the power to say *no*. But give yourself permission to say *yes* to what you do want. Guide your partner. Do not assume the other person can read your mind or your body or that you will be seen as "demanding" for expressing what pleases you. It is amazing how often marriage counselors and sex therapists hear one or the other partner say, "If he (she) had only *told* me what he (she) likes!"

The frequency of making love is individual. People too often place emphasis on how *often* and not enough on how *satisfying* the lovemaking. This can harm a relationship mentally and spiritually. Making love should be a tender, treasured act, experienced at times right for both partners, not a boring, monotonous repetition. Sometimes, when two people are holistically attuned to each other, the frequency of the sex act may actually be lessened, because of the overwhelming surge of energy and joy it generates for longer periods of time. Ideal lovemaking lasts as long as it can, so that both partners are fulfilled, happy, and satisfied.

A strong sex drive is, of course, necessary for the propagation of the race, but remember that *obsession* with the physical self harms the spiritual self. It is vitally important that, when striving for a holistic lifestyle, you make sure these areas are balanced. Exercising and eating properly will do wonders for your sex life. Neglecting these factors affects both your interpersonal relationships and your sexual functioning: A person constantly tired because of indiscriminate eating, drinking, and taking drugs cannot carry on a meaningful relationship with anyone, let alone make passionate love. Finally, getting in touch with yourself through meditation and prayer can help you be the most you can be.

CELIBACY

I was totally celibate for a period of my life. The strict yogis believe in this practice or in sex for procreative purposes only. I went for two years without having any form of sexual activity, a period during which I was involved with a group of people who believed that sexual energy detracts from spiritual evolution and slows down the evolutionary process. Sexual energy (called *kundalini* in Eastern terminology) is supposedly housed in the *root chakra* (a spiritual center located in the genital area) and can be channeled through other *chakras*, or spiritual centers, to the *crown chakra* located at the top of the head. Each chakra has specific energy as well as correlations with specific mental, emotional, and spiritual states. I was taught that, through the opening of this center, one could achieve Nirvana, a state of spiritual bliss.

At that time, I wanted to do whatever I could to develop more of my psychic and spiritual awareness, and I felt I could mentally and spiritually handle controlling my sexual desires with my will. I had always considered myself a strongly sexual person, so this was a challenging experience. Only by being around other people with the same lifestyle—celibate vegetarians—was I able to divert my sexual energy to other activities. I meditated and prayed a lot, especially when I had these "urges." I concentrated on the *kundalini* spiritual energy opening up my psychic/spiritual centers.

After a time, I grew accustomed to not thinking about sex and even thought it ridiculous for others to be so interested in it, especially when it caused so many problems for them. But I ended my celibacy in 1981 and also changed my vegetarian diet to a mixed-food diet. This decision came because I had realized no overwhelming change in my psychic/spiritual awareness, and because I had met someone with whom I wanted to have a relationship.

From my experience with celibacy, I learned that sex for the right reasons *with the right, holistic person* does not interfere with psychic/spiritual ability. In fact, my own spiritual abilities have continued to progress since that time. Celibacy should not be attempted by everyone. Many people are not able to redirect their sexual energies and could even become emotionally or mentally unbalanced by such an attempt. Many religions still require celibacy—some only at certain times of the year—and many people accept it and are comfortable with it in that context.

A great deal of shock was expressed when, a few years ago, Ann Landers was flooded with letters supporting the desire of one correspondent who said she'd be happy to forgo the sex act and just be held close and hugged instead. In fact, more letters were received by the newspaper on that one subject than had ever been tallied before. Psychologists, commenting on the phenomenon, voiced dismay that so many women were crying out for a closeness and tenderness that eluded them in their sexual relations.

Celibacy is not the natural human state, and for the majority of the human population it is not a considered option. Given this fact, it becomes even more important that we do everything in our power to make the potentially most exalted form of human communication a pleasurable and uplifting experience.

Chapter Three

OTHER RELATIONSHIPS

THE PARENT-CHILD RELATIONSHIP

Parents' feelings and attitudes can greatly affect a child's future sexuality. Telling your five-year-old that he shouldn't touch his private parts because they're bad, or that he cannot sleep in the same room with his twin sister because boys and girls are different and shouldn't be together, will probably cause sexual confusion as the child grows up.

Parental influence does not end with specific, spoken words. Children are marked both positively and negatively by the whole household environment. A girl growing up in a male-dominated family may feel subservient around all males, while a girl raised with respect and responsibilities will be more capable of dealing with men on an equal basis.

Children learn most of their life patterns in the first two-to-five years of life. In a way, monitoring the first five years of a child's life is like programming a computer. If the input is a loving environment, the output will be a reflection of that. If the input is hateful, the child will be full of anger and will have many disturbances.

Studies have shown that a fetus reacts not only to what the mother eats and drinks (including drugs) but also to her emotions. Traumatic experiences during pregnancy can adversely affect a fetus, leading to problems as the child matures. Conversely, many women are convinced that speaking lovingly to the fetus creates a calmer, happier baby.

Based on my observations as a schoolteacher and private counselor, I strongly believe that a child raised in a spiritual environment is less likely to have emotional and behavioral problems. I recall a plaque that hung in our kitchen when I was a child, which read, "The family that prays together stays together." I firmly believe that to be true, but I would add that the family must not only pray but *believe* in the power of prayer. The particular religion one chooses doesn't matter. Meditation and prayer are universal. People united by spiritual goals create a more loving and harmonious environment for all.

Most families don't spend enough quality time together, meditating and praying, to learn to love each other completely. They lack the spiritual commitment to each other and to God. Remember, it is the quality, not the quantity of time that matters most. If a child is in an unhappy home and feels unloved, even being with a parent twenty-four hours a day won't make things better. On the other hand, think of how much easier your own life would have been had you learned as a child the things you have read in this book.

All children should be helped to acquire a basic understanding of and belief in a Higher Intelligence or divine God-force that flows throughout the universe. Children need a sense of security and guidance. Discipline and reassurance are essential in order for the child to grow and develop the ultimate independence you wish him to attain.

When I give psychic readings, questions frequently arise regarding parent-child problems. I tell the parents to have realistic expectations. Even if you provide the best education, all the comforts of life, a positive and religious environment, and security and consistency, children can still disappoint you. Peer pressure, the outside environment, accidents you can't control, all have their effect on children. In addition, their goals may not fit yours. Speak realistically with your children. Always be honest with them, and try to relate to them on a level they understand. Remember the way you saw things at that age, and remember that you are there to be a *parent*, not a *friend*. Tell them about holistic principles at an early age, monitor their diet and exercise as you do your own, and—above all—set a good example.

Operate on the theory that—as in school—there is no such thing as a stupid question. Every question deserves an answer—and an *honest* answer, at that. *Never* laugh at or brush off a child's question. That might be the *last* question he ever asks you. Give your child an explanation he can understand, but never make him think he's too stupid or you're too busy for proper answers.

Erratic or violent behavior in children, even learning disabilities, may be caused by metabolic disorders or allergies. If you notice unusual or negative behavior patterns, have your child tested by one of the many professionals in this field. I recall a story that brought tears to my eyes, regarding a young boy with an attention disorder. He said to his mother, "My body won't let me sit still and pay attention, in class. What can I do to help it behave?" A change in his diet brought the desired results.

Children are not like dolls that can be left alone till the next time you're ready to play. Bearing children carries great responsibilities—physical, emotional, and financial. Think carefully about your readiness to assume these responsibilities before bringing a child into the world.

DISCIPLINE

Discipline is one of the most important factors in life. Without it, there can be no sustained learning, no productivity, no progress, no gain. Children certainly need discipline—at home, at school, and in sports—but meting out discipline means more than just punishment. Think of it, rather, as a learning process.

The best way to establish discipline is through communication. If a parent is firm but loving, the child generally will respond, if he understands the reasoning behind the parent's request or directive. Yelling is one of the *least* effective modes of communicating, as the tone and loudness interfere with the message. Be very clear about your expectations, when setting ground rules for children. They should not be expected to know everything or do everything right all the time, but they should be taught the difference between right and wrong and the consequences of their wrong behavior.

If communication fails, check for physiological or medical problems. I know of a hearing-impaired child whose parents were unaware of the problem and thought their child was simply ignoring their requests. He, of course, didn't understand why he was being punished, as he didn't know he was doing anything wrong.

When physiological reasons have been ruled out, restrictions or limitations of freedom are highly effective forms of discipline. Avoid hitting a child, as that teaches him a lesson of a different sort. Mild force should be used only as a last resort. Always explain to your children the reason for disciplinary action, and make sure to point out that it is the *behavior*, not the *child*, you find unacceptable. Under *no* circumstances should you ever tell a child he is bad or impossible. Statements of that nature are implanted in the subconscious mind forever. I remember actually seeing a little boy wince, when his parent—referring to an *illness*—made the mistake of saying, "No one's as bad as *he* is."

One of the most important jobs of parenthood is instilling a sense of self-esteem in one's children. A person with high self-esteem is not afraid to ask questions, because he's not afraid of seeming stupid; he is not easily led because his self-esteem gives him a sense of independence; he is not subject to high-pressure salesmanship because those tactics are designed to make people *feel* better than they *believe* they are; and he's not afraid to say he was wrong, because he knows there is no shame in it. All vibrations between family members affect everyone in the family. A child's bad behavior can affect the vibratory harmony of a marriage, which in turn affects the way in which children are treated by each of the parents. When disharmony settles into a family—especially when the parents disagree—children frequently pull away from the nucleus, rebel against authority, and lose respect for the parents as they play one against the other.

It is extremely important to teach a child limits. Problems can develop at a *very* young age—younger than most parents realize a child's mental capacity. Studies have shown that some criminal personalities developed as early as age five. Do not underestimate the intelligence or perceptive ability of young children. They, too, have an intuitive sense or right and wrong and expect you to enforce the proper code of behavior.

ABUSE IN THE FAMILY

When a child becomes a problem and the parent cannot deal with the child in a rational manner, some parents turn to violence, often unprovoked. No one knows the exact figures for child abuse, as crimes of this nature often go unreported, but estimates range from three to eight million cases per year. Many victims of abuse choose not to report it, due to feelings of shame, embarrassment, and guilt. This is especially true of spouse abuse.

In recent years, increased awareness and publicity has resulted in a rise in the number or reported cases, indicating that many victims no longer are willing to be brutalized. They also are finding comfort and support in groups designed to assist, specifically, abused children, battered wives, and victims of incest and rape.

Although there is no excusing abuse, one can discern a common pattern in the background of abusers: Most were, themselves, raised in an abusive environment. Sociologist Richard Giles of the University of Rhode Island says, "The husband will beat his wife. The wife may then learn to beat the children. The bigger siblings learn it is okay to hit the little ones, and the family pet may be the ultimate recipient of violence."

Most rapists, it has been learned, were sexually abused as children. Studies of prison populations show that 90 percent of all inmates were abused children. Among children who have grown up seeing their mothers abused, the boys are prone to become wife beaters and the girls are prone to become abused wives. But the girls also become abusers in their own right. Among the sexually abused, girls tend to choose abusive husbands, while boys frequently become pedophiles (adults sexually attracted to children) or rapists. A pedophile is rarely rehabilitated.

It may surprise some to learn that women are more likely to abuse children than men, since women spend more time with their children. The stress that accompanies child rearing, and the financial burdens placed on parents with children, sometimes exacerbates the situation. If the child is unwanted, retarded, physically handicapped, or even extremely intelligent, he or she runs an even greater risk of abuse than a normal child. In the case of abusive male adults (father, stepfather, mother's lover or friend), the man might not just beat the child but also sexually abuse him or her. The physical and emotional scars of such abuse can last a lifetime, and it is imperative that such children get counseling, even if they have grown into adulthood.

FRIENDSHIPS

According to the Law of Magnetic Attraction, "like attracts like," so we are bound to draw friends to us who reflect our own vibrations. Our association with people who are more spiritually and holistically attuned and whose vibrations are at a level higher than our own increases our holistic health. I myself have evolved to the point that I believe in spiritually loving everyone but in associating closely only with those who know and love God and who have positive thoughts.

Do not concern yourself with or concentrate on negative emotions sustained in prior friendships or relationships. It is not only *un*productive; it can be *counter*productive, as it can ruin the friendships you have today. You must be free of the past in order to live profitably in the present. The most difficult test of controlled thoughts and emotions is sending love and positive thoughts to those who have injured us. Ask God to show you how to resolve a problem you're having with a friend (or lover, or parent, or child, or colleague) and then forget the situation. Never harbor negative feelings or hatred toward anyone. It is best to put such situations out of your mind. A fine little book that deals with such problems and gives a number of excellent possible solutions is *How to Forgive When You Don't Know How*, by Jacqui Bishop and Mary Grunte.

As with lovers, spouses, and children, do not be overpossessive with friends, and don't expect them to agree with you all the time. Don't become angry when their plans don't coincide with yours, or if they choose to be with others when you'd like to be with them. Being overdemanding doesn't nurture good friendship. Obviously, if they choose to be apart from you more than with you, it may signal a need to reevaluate the relationship. But generally, it is best to take a "live and let live" attitude: Live your life and let your friends live theirs. Remember, too, that everyone makes mistakes and sometimes people hurt you, but holding grudges benefits no one. If a person's intentions are good and genuine, it is always better to let things cool off for a while. Then, it is easier to make up without recriminations. This holds for all kinds of personal relationships.

With a person who has hurt you intentionally, you may find a different tack more useful and helpful. As Bishop and Grunte point out, the sad fact is that your anger hurts *you* (both physically and emotionally) more than it bothers the one who has harmed you. If, instead of focusing *anger* on the person in question, you send love and blessings and ask God to help him *evolve*, you accomplish a double mission: You insure your own mental and physical health and well-being and you foster a change in the behavior of someone who needs to change. Moreover, since what you put out comes back to you, *you* yourself will benefit from increased love and blessings. In this way, you can turn what, otherwise, might be a devastating experience into a "win-win" situation. This is the power which God has given us and which, if you ask, He will help you to put to good use.

WORK RELATIONSHIPS

Work not only sustains us financially, it gives direction and discipline to our lives. Even if you have a dull job and desire to get a better one, don't be negative about your current position. Learn what you can from it and work toward bettering it. Never consider that you work only for pay: There is always something more to be learned from work.

Believe it or not, problems on the job can be a blessing in disguise. They can trigger a positive change in your life. Be grateful for them and learn from them, remembering that we learn more from our failures than from success. A television interviewer once told me about the horrors of her first show. Her questions were interesting, and her guest *should* have been, but he gave her only "Yes" and "No" answers. It was like pulling teeth to get more information from him.

Fortunately, a fellow professional and friend of this young woman was watching the program and phoned her immediately afterward. "Did you talk with that man about what you were going to discuss on the air, before you went on?" she asked. "Of course," replied the young woman. "That was your mistake," her friend told her. "Talk about the weather, children, or favorite sports to relax a guest, but *never* discuss the issues. If you do, he'll think he has to come up with *new* ideas, on the air, and if he has none, he will freeze." The young woman followed her advice and never had that problem again. Telling me this story, she said, "If I had done everything right the first time, I might never have learned that important lesson. Making that mistake has made me a far better interviewer, and I have passed that advice on to many others as well."

Make every attempt to solve your problems, and look for the good or positive that can come from an apparently negative situation. Think of the factors that caused the problem and then of the positive steps you can take to overcome it and get started on a new, more successful course. Rid yourself of any fears, or negative emotions that might get in your way. Sometimes doing what you had initially feared most leads to the greatest success. It certainly leads to the greatest sense of satisfaction.

AMBITION

Everyone has dreams of doing something special with his or her life. While some dreams are loftier than others, having goals is important in stimulating our spiritual evolution. You don't have to work in a place of worship to be working for God. Any honest job well done is acceptable in His eyes.

Your ambition and skill will determine how far you go in your chosen profession. Successful people are, typically, quick-minded and quick-moving, and their confidence is infectious. This comes from an attitude of knowing what they want and a willingness to work as hard as necessary to get there. Many motivational speakers believe that, in order to accomplish something outstanding, one must be prepared to sacrifice in other areas of life. When you read of the lifestyles of Olympic athletes and foreign correspondents for the world's leading newspapers—especially in areas of conflict—you know this to be fact. Each person must decide for himself what is most important to him.

It does not necessarily follow that having a low ambition level will result in failure. In fact, too *much* ambition can cause unhappiness and dissatisfaction with yourself and everything around you. Ambition is directly related to the amount of emphasis you put on your job and how you see it as a reflection of yourself. Some people are totally consumed by their work and see their lives defined by it; others have a nine-to-five job that pays the rent but means little else to them. The latter group tend to have ambitions for other types of gains in life.

WORKING WITH OTHER EMPLOYEES

Getting along well with people on the job makes your life more pleasant and rewarding. Negative people are to be found in all areas of life, and the workplace is no exception, but while you cannot avoid these people entirely, you can make it a point to stay away from them as much as possible. Try to be neutral and cool in your feelings toward them, and remain positive at all times, even when you are forced to disagree.

There are constructive ways to argue a point. Always seek those paths, as unemotional discussions are much better for working out problems than are heated arguments. When emotions flare, stress is compounded. And stress causes any number of health problems. Once again, this goes for personal as well as work relationships.

BEING THE BOSS

Work relationships are extremely complicated, especially when job placement is determined by factors other than merit alone.

In any supervisory position, it is vital to motivate people properly. When everyone is happy and productive, it reflects better on the boss. For best results:

1. Let people know you have trust and confidence in them. If any employee is not working to your satisfaction, speak with him or her. Communication is the best way to deal with problems. Encourage your employees to tell you if personal problems are affecting their work, but don't become involved with their problems.

2. Treat your employees as fellow human beings, not as machines, lower-class people, or sex objects.

3. Be diplomatic at all times. Look at all sides of a question or problem brought to your attention. Don't play favorites.

4. Be calm and cool when you reprimand someone, and don't let your emotions make your decisions for you. Emotions are not rational and, therefore, aren't appropriate guides for decision-making. Yelling and name-calling lowers people's self-esteem and causes resentment.

The late Max Karl, founder of Mortgage Guaranty Insurance Corporation, a *Fortune* 500 company, told of his dismay at hearing the head of another of the country's major corporations express pride in having cut his labor force by 10 percent, with no considerations other than "downsizing" the company to reduce costs. In Karl's opinion, "a company head should think about humanitarian needs, especially if it doesn't affect the bottom line too much. You may save $2 million," he says, "but that's really $1 million after taxes, and if the company does $135 million annually, what difference does $1 million make? When you think about the number of families being supported by those employees, why is it so important to have another $1 million to return to the stockholders? With ten million stockholders, that's only *ten cents each!* It's better to have a company with high morale and to find other ways to make up for the loss of income. It insures a better work environment and greater dedication from employees, if they know the boss has their best interests at heart." This goes for mid-range executives, as well, many of whom are in their late forties or early fifties and would elsewhere be considered unemployable for being "too old": As he explained, "If they know that company policy is to be loyal to them, as long as they are performing well, it will certainly show in their performance." It should come as no surprise to learn that Karl's files were filled with letters of admiration and gratitude and that the company, under his direction, was so successful. One major characteristic of successful business people is a strong intuitive sense. Knowing who is going to help you—and who will hinder your efforts—is a tremendous advantage, especially in a supervisory role. In addition, intuition is extremely helpful in hiring employees. Sometimes you can pick up vibrations from a person by shaking hands. The firmness of a handshake is always revealing. (Beware the person who grabs your hand and throws you off balance.) Both the boss and the potential employee should be acutely aware of the energy flow and eye contact, when meeting for the first time. Pay attention to "body language." A number of excellent and useful books have been written on this subject. Look for the positive, in others, but beware of the syndrome in which there is a "triumph of hope over experience." Meditate and "program" for your goals beforehand. This will not only give you confidence; it will help ensure the desired outcome.

Appendix

Some Final Thoughts on the Body and Soul

The doctor of the future will give no medicine, but will interest his patients in the care of the human frame, in diet, and in the cause and prevention of disease.

—THOMAS A. EDISON

Let food be your medicine, and medicine be your food.

—HIPPOCRATES

Your first duty is to make the body healthy. Without health, nothing can be achieved. Not only higher goals, but even worldly success is based on your health, your condition.

—SWAMI SATCHIDANANDA

Physician, heal thyself.

—LUKE 4:23

A sound mind in a healthy body.

—SENECA

MY PHILOSOPHY ON HEALTH

The body is a vehicle for the spirit to express itself. When the body is clean inside, the mind becomes clearer and the spirit within can manifest itself more freely, resulting in a balanced energy flow. Unfortunately, most people spend more time, care, and effort keeping their cars in tune than they do their bodies.

Balancing your body will make you a healthier, more spiritual person. But balance is not to be confused with moderation. The statements, "Everything is fine in moderation" and "Be moderate in all things" can, if taken literally, be detrimental to your holistic health. Moderation is different for different people: What is moderate to some is excessive to others. People have varying requirements, tolerances, and allergies. For one person, a single aspirin may be beneficial; another may require two or three; yet another may have bleeding ulcers and not be able to tolerate aspirin at all. By the same token, sleep patterns and requirements vary widely, as do the ability to tolerate alcohol, caffeine, and sugar.

It makes sense to assume that if your body is healthy it is easier to be more spiritual. If you are ill or in pain, it is certainly more difficult to help yourself, let alone concentrate on helping others. In poor health it is hard to be motivated to do very much at all—even to pray or meditate effectively.

As your nutritional understanding and healthful practices become more routine, you will gain more control over your health and body. Holistic health education, combined with self-discipline and patience, will continue to pay great holistic health dividends for years to come. Overwhelming evidence has begun to accumulate indicating that many disorders can be prevented or significantly influenced through what are now being called "preventive measures." And health care practitioners and providers finally are recognizing that *preventive* medicine is cheaper than *curative* medicine.

Holistic medicine (preventive health care) is based on the metaphysical belief that body, mind, and spirit all are integrated. Incorporated into this concept of *holism* is also a belief in a higher intelligence and in the effectiveness of the power of prayer and spirituality. All health-influencing dimensions are explored with the patient: mental, physical, and emotional. Therapy is rendered accordingly, to restore and maintain health. Spiritual love plays an essential role in the holistic approach, which incorporates preventive, alternative, and traditional health care methods. Holistic, then, refers to the whole person, within the context of his whole life and complete environment. (The term originally was spelled *wholistic,* to reflect this orientation.) By building a physically strong body through exercise and nutritionally balancing the body chemistry through proper diet, you can develop an immune system that will help fend off disease.

Fatigue is one of the major complaints in our society. It is one of the primary symptoms in thousands of physical disorders and a wide variety of mental disturbances. Fatigue due to boredom or depression often can be cured with an exercise regimen. It is now widely known that a walk after meals (like the ones our grandparents took!) is beneficial to both physical and mental functioning, and that retirees who undergo regular exercise live longer, healthier, and more productive lives than those who are sedentary.

More books and magazines are sold promoting diets than any other single topic. Everyone seeks the miracle or the secret to losing weight, looking great, and feeling fit—usually with little or no effort. But we all know that *that* solution does not exist. Slowly, we have come to learn that not *diets* but *habits* are what count, and the habits that insure long and healthy life emphasize light meals of fruits, vegetables, complex carbohydrates, a little fat, and protein; regular exercise; fresh air; and a positive mental outlook.

In spite of the numbers of people who exercise to exhaustion or run twenty-six-mile marathons, most of us will keep our bodies in shape and in tune with a regular program of nonstrenuous walking. Water exercise (a variety of movements done in a swimming pool) has become quite popular and appears to be equally beneficial, in addition to helping avoid the heat and areas considered unsafe for walking. If you want a machine to help you, this opinion from an exercise specialist is worth remembering: "The best piece of equipment," he told me, "is the one you will use. Garages across the country are filled with no-longer-used stationary bicycles. Cross-country ski machines will give you a great workout, but only if you use them. Studies show that the one piece of equipment still in use, after twenty years, is the treadmill." Part of what makes treadmills so attractive is the ability to use them at any time, in any weather, and to adjust them for both speed and incline if you want to increase the workout. Their popularity also has brought the price down to a level far below the cost of health clubs—or doctors!

The importance of proper diet and exercise is also related to the control of stress. Stress is one of our society's greatest health concerns, for although a certain amount of stress is necessary for any living thing to function optimally, life in the twentieth century has produced more than a fair share. The holistic approach to stress management emphasizes meditation, physical exercise, prayer, nutrition, and positive thinking. When a stressful situation occurs, try not to panic. Stop and think. Meditate and relax. Numerous studies have shown that meditation produces a state of restful awareness and positive changes in heart rate and oxygen consumption. Those who meditate indicate they can handle stress better, when it occurs; they are more emotionally stable and have more energy and enthusiasm. Special prayers, included daily, will help you through any stressful period, as will the visualization techniques mentioned in earlier chapters.

Finally, remember to care for specific parts of your body: Your eyes, ears, teeth, skin, nails and hair require the same attention you give your inner organs. "Glowing" good health is not just an expression: With proper care and practice, you will actually *radiate* a physical state of wellness.

A recent government study revealed that one-third of all medical visits in the United States involve some sort of alternative medicine. In contrast to what was true only a decade ago, much of the Western medical establishment is now recognizing the benefits and validity of what used to be known as *folk medicine*. Even the National Institutes of Health, our government's primary medical research institution in Washington, has created a Department of Alternative Medicine to study these theories and practices.

While much of what we have read in the past has been purely "anecdotal" (one person's experience), more and more strictly scientific studies are confirming what ancient and so-called "primitive" peoples have known for hundreds and even thousands of years. The use of garlic as a preventative and moldy bread (later developed as penicillin!) as a cure are but two—from ancient Greece.

The literature on these practices and studies expands daily, as does the number of practitioners. Major medical schools publish newsletters, print and broadcast journalists produce more and more features on the subject for prime-time viewing, and we all stand to benefit from our increased knowledge. Even the mind-body connection was highlighted in Bill Moyers's television series, *Healing and the Mind*.

As we look forward to the twenty-first century, we are learning not to ignore those who have lived—and learned—before.

THE NATURE OF THE SOUL

The payment of karmic debts concerns the transformation of the soul, not of the physical body. While ailments of a physical nature can be ways of paying debts, they are not a direct way but an indication of higher knowledge that will be gained only after we pass into other lives. When you are sick, it is a form of teaching, a sign that you should pay more attention to other aspects of your life that you were possibly overlooking.

Your body is the temple of your soul and therefore should be kept in optimum condition, but it is the soul itself that is of supreme importance. The soul is formless, spaceless, and timeless. In a different "dimension" from the solid, physical body of man, it grows and matures with us, and it cannot be destroyed, only transformed into a higher state. In other words, this is the part of our existence that is immortal.

MY DEFINITION OF "HOLISTIC"

H Health, as in total fitness
O Optimum achievement, as in job fulfillment
L Love, as in ideal companionship
I Inspiration, as in divine motivation
S Spirituality, as in oneness with the God-force
T Tranquillity, as in peace of mind
I Illumination, as in self-realization
C Courage, as in self-reliance

CREATE YOUR OWN FUTURE!

Now that you have read of all the glorious possibilities for your life, it is up to you to put what you have learned into effect. All the learning in the world is for naught if the lessons learned go unapplied.

You know, now, that you can, indeed, *create your own future.* The second part of the equation is that *you must take responsibility for your life.* Just as a psychic knows *where* you are going but not *how* you will get there, so this book has provided you with a map, a compass, and the driving lessons, but not with the car. It is up to *you* to decide where you will go, when, and in what fashion.

Always remember the Universal Laws and that ignorance of them is no excuse: They remain operative whether or not you know about them, and whether or not you choose to ignore them. If you find you are not getting what you want, go back to the chapter and discussion of the Laws, and consider that you may have to reapply one or more of them.

You cannot do things halfway, just as it often is said you can't be "a *little bit* pregnant." Set yourself a code of moral behavior and stick to it for as long as you find it guiding you in the path you wish to travel. Don't be afraid to adjust that code: None of us is perfect, and we all make mistakes. Some mistakes are due simply to inexperience, explaining why the expression "experience is the best teacher" is used so often. Be flexible and be understanding of yourself, as you expect to be of others.

Be aware, always, of the mind-body connection. Life is *integrated,* and your physical and emotional lives are as one. You are developing a *whole* person: aware, centered, and growing spiritually with each passing day and experience. God (or whatever spirit force you choose), your guardian angels, and your spirit guides are there to assist you. Do not treat them frivolously, for they will serve you as you implore them. ("Be careful what you ask for; you might get it.") *Trust* that they are there for you, and they will be. And be open to the many ways in which they may send you messages and assistance.

Remember that you have a responsibility to others, as well as to yourself. Being *centered* in the universe does not mean being *self-centered.* Your goal is to become a spiritual, holistic person at peace with yourself and with the universe. All the good you do *will* come back to you—if not in this lifetime, then in the next. But rest assured that it will come back.

Creative Visualization is one of your most important tools. Use it wisely and well. A positive outlook—and surrounding yourself with positive people—are essential to your success and eventually will become an almost automatic response, in your new, holistic way of life.

As you become more perceptive and aware, you will become your own psychic, making your own analyses and predictions. But this may take quite some time, so do not be impatient: Washing the windows is the last thing you do after you get the house in order. In the meantime, there are other people and other ways to help you receive divine answers. Seek them out and discover which ones work best for you.

And always remember to praise God.

BIBLIOGRAPHY

Biermann, June, and Barbara Toohey. *The Woman's Wholistic Headache Relief Book.* New York: J. P. Tarcher, Inc., 1979.

Burroughs, Stanley. *Healing for the Age of Enlightenment.* Kailua, Hawaii: Stanley Burroughs Publishing, 1976.

Cayce, Hugh Lynn. *The Edgar Cayce Reader No. 2.* New York: Paperback Library, 1969.

Chatsworth, Colin, and Loren Chatsworth. *The Great Calcium Myth.* Charlottesville, Va.: Chatsworth Publishing, 1984.

Cherlin, Andrew, and Frank F. Furstenberg, Jr. "The American Family in the Year of 2000." *The Futurist* (June 1983).

Cirincion, Barbara, and Dr. Arthur Evans. *Total Dental Health.* Manhattan Beach, Calif.: New Age Publishing, 1979.

Cox, Cynthia. "Lost or Found." *Fort Lauderdale News,* July 25, 1982, pp. 1E and 3E.

Davis, James. "A Controversial Bible Story." *Fort Lauderdale Sun-Sentinel,* June 18, 1984, pp. 1D and 4D.

Ferguson, Marilyn. *The Brain Revolution.* New York: Taplinger Publishing, 1978.

Gettings, Fred. *The Book of Tarot.* London, Eng.: Triune Books, 1973.

Graham, Billy. *Angels.* Garden City, N.Y.: Doubleday, 1975.

Graham, Henry G. *Where We Got the Bible.* Hawthorne, Calif.: Book Club of America, 1977.

Gray, Eden. *A Complete Guide to the Tarot.* New York: Bantam, 1983.

Heany, John J. *The Sacred and the Psychic.* Ramsey, N.J.: Paulist Press, 1984.

Hoffman, Wendell H. *Using Energy to Heal.* Wendell Hoffman Publishing, 1979.

Johnson, Julian P. *The Path of the Masters.* Delhi, India: National Printing Works, 1939.

Kotulak, Ronald. "Sex Isn't Just Normal: It's Good For You, Too." *Miami Herald.* September 29, 1981, pp. 1C and 3C.

———. "Still a Nation of Sexual Illiterates." *Miami Herald,* September 28, 1981, pp. 1C and 2C.

Kraft, Dean. *Portrait of a Psychic Healer.* New York: G. P. Putnam's Sons, 1981.

Kulivinskas, Viktoras H. *Survival into the 21st Century.* Werchersfield, Conn.: Omangod Press, 1975.

Kunz, Kevin, and Barbara Kunz. *A Complete Guide to Foot Reflexology.* Albuquerque, N. Mex.: Reflex Research Project, 1981.

Leo, John. "Sex and the Married Woman." *Time,* January 31, 1983.

Longest, Ernest S. *Meditation Techniques.* Rockford, Va.: Common Wealth Press, 1971.

Magnuson, Ed. "Child Abuse: The Ultimate Betrayal." *Time,* September 5, 1983.

Maltz, Maxwell. *Psycho-Cybernetics.* New York, N.Y.: Prentice-Hall, 1960.

McRae, Ronald. *Mind Wars.* New York: St. Martin's Press, 1984.

Meek, George W. *From Enigma to Science*, vol. 1. Wheaton, Ill.: Theosophical Publishing House, 1977.

———. *Healers and the Healing Process*. Wheaton, Ill.: Theosophical Publishing House, 1977.

Moody, Raymond A., Jr. *Life after Life*. Covington, Ga.: Mockingbird Books, 1975.

Moss, Thelma, and John Hubacher. "The Nature of Kirlian Photography." Palisades, Calif.: Prism Center.

Murphy, Joseph. *How to Use Your Healing Powers*. Santa Monica, Calif.: Deross and Co., 1974.

———. *The Power of Your Subconscious Mind*. Englewood Cliffs, N.J.: Prentice-Hall, 1963.

Murphy, Wendy. *Dealing with Headaches*. Alexandria, Va.: Time-Life Books, 1982.

Nara, Robert O., D.D.S., and Steven, Mariner. *How to Become Dentally Self-Sufficient*. Houghton, Mich.: Oramedics International Press, 1995.

———. *Money—By the Mouthful*. Houghton, Mich.: Oramedics International Press, 1979.

Norvell, Anthony. *Meta-Physics*. West Nyack, N.Y.: Parker Publishing, 1973.

O'Neil, Geri. *Super Self: Life Without Limits*. Slingerlands, N.Y.: Richelieu Court, 1984.

Oski, Frank A., M.D. *Don't Drink Your Milk!* Syracuse, N.Y.: Mollica Press, 1983.

Pearson, Durk, and Sandy Shaw. *Life Extension*. New York: Warner Books, 1982.

Phillips, Deborah, with Robert Judd. *How to Fall Out of Love*. New York: Fawcett Popular Library, 1978.

Quinn, Arthur Vincent. *Cancer Interferon Foundation Diet*. Santa Barbara, Calif.: Arthur Vincent Quinn Publishing, 1984.

Rehert, Isaac. "Sex Roles in the Three Year Old: Clearing Confusion at an Early Age." *Psychology Today*, October 1982.

Rubinstein, Carl. "The Modern Art of Courtly Love." *Psychology Today*, July 1983.

Sampsidis, Nicholas. *Homogenized Milk and Atherosclerosis Cause and Effect*. Glen Head, N.Y.: Sunflower Publishing, 1981.

Schult, Bill. *The Psychic Frontiers of Medicine*. New York: Fawcett World Library, 1977.

Schultz, William. *Shiatsu*. New York: Bell Publishing, 1976.

Shook, Edward E. *Advanced Treatises in Herbology*. Lakemount, Ga.: C.S.A. Printing and Bindery, 1978.

Targ, Russell, and Keith Harary, *The Mind Race*. New York: Villard Books, 1984.

Tavris, Carol. "The Myth of the 50–50 Marriage." *Woman's Day*, March 1984, pp. 47–48.

The World Almanac. *The World Almanac of Strange*. New York: New American Library, 1977.

Urantia Foundation, *The Urantia Book*. Chicago: Urantia Foundation, 1955.

Weed, Joseph J. *Wisdom of the Mystic Masters*. New York: Parker Publishing 1970.

INDEX